THE HOW AND WHY:
Taking Care of Business with the Enneagram

A Practical Organization Development Framework as Bridge and Foundation to Drive more Effective, Efficient, and Sustainable Business Results and Relationships

Second Edition

R. Karl Hebenstreit, Ph.D.

Front Cover picture by R. Karl Hebenstreit
Front and Rear Cover Design by Robin C. Grant
Back Cover (biography) picture by Ken Sergi

Copyright 2021
Published by Perform and Function, LLC

Table of Contents

Acknowledgements v

Chapter 1 | Sense-Making. 1
Chapter 2 | Introducing the Enneagram into Business Settings 6
Chapter 3 | Recruitment, Engagement, and Retention . . 23
Chapter 4 | Strategic Planning. 40
Chapter 5 | Values. 50
Chapter 6 | Culture 60
Chapter 7 | Decision-Making, Problem-Solving, and Innovation 69
Chapter 8 | Influence 78
Chapter 9 | Communication, Communication, Communication 88
Chapter 10 | Executive Coaching and Development . . . 102
Chapter 11 | Team-Building. 153
Chapter 12 | Change Management 174
Chapter 13 | Accountability 188
Chapter 14 | Conflict Management 190
Chapter 15 | The Process Enneagram and Organization Design 208
Chapter 16 | The Enneagram in Agility 213

Epilogue 219
Appendix A | You Know You're Accessing Enneagram
              Type ... If/When 221
Appendix B | Enneagram Types, Subtypes, Counter-Types,
              and Look-Alikes. 222
Appendix C | The Enneagram with MBTI, DiSC, and Body
              Center Correlates. 223
Appendix D | Behavioral Interview Questions to Assess
              Emotional Intelligence. 224
Appendix E | Methods of Enneagram Type Identification
              ("Typing"). 225
Appendix F | Facilitation Success Guidelines 228
Table of Figures 229
References and Additional Resources 232

Acknowledgements

Many people must be credited for leading me to the Enneagram and its power of creating understanding, compassion, and clarity, and to the ultimate creation of this work. First and foremost, my parents, Domna and Jim, who have provided me with constant love and support in everything I do, and who placed such a great emphasis on and interest in my education. Special thanks to my mother for contributing her professional editing skills and advice to this work. Continuing education led me to discover the Enneagram during the course of my graduate studies at the California School of Professional Psychology, and for that I must credit Dr. Jo Sanzgiri, who invited the inimitable Helen Palmer to introduce the Enneagram to our class. My dissertation advisers, Dr. Benisa Berry, Dr. Maurice Monette, and Dr. Mary Bast were instrumental and supportive in the completion of my research and thesis work. My involvement in the Enneagram community has enriched, furthered, and honed my comprehension of the Enneagram – for that I must specifically thank Claire Barnum, Katherine Chernick-Fauvre, Dr. Beatrice Chestnut, Dirk Cloete, Linda Fadden, Kathryn

Grant, Russ Hudson, Andrea Isaacs, Patrick Kayrooz, Dr. Ginger Lapid-Bogda, Maria José Munita, Dr. Deborah Ooten, Helen Palmer, Ken Sergi, Mario Sikora, Sean Smith, Elizabeth Wagele, and Dr. Earl Wagner, along with the countless other researchers, theorists, thinkers, and founders of the greater Enneagram community. A special shout out goes to the Canadian (Rob Fitzel, Ruth Shell, David Sie, and Dr. Penny Whillans, among so many others), and European (Rebecka Bartolomé, Antonio Cordeiro, Dr. C.J. Fitzsimons, Mette Hvied Lauesen, Cecilia Alwin Mattson, and Claus Roager Olsen, among so many others) Enneagram community members, all of whom have been generously receptive and encouraging of my work and the development of this book to disseminate it even further. The Enneagram community also introduced me to Robin Grant, who keeps me grounded and authentic in my work, and with whom I continue to grow, learn, and develop. And his mad graphic design and artistic skills are on full display on this edition's book cover, along with his and Maxwell Kolb's impressive work on the new layout and tables! My deepest gratitude and appreciation go to all my friends and colleagues who have put up with my passion (some might even say compulsion?!) around this system and my use of it in our everyday and business lives; thank you especially to Rachael Allison, Dick Anderson, Christine Barnes, Kirstin Barton, Monique Bobadilla, Tasheena Braxton, Donna Carter, Andrew Chandler, Yuwen Chu, Darby Davenport, Pam Dewar, Lindsey "Randazzl" Doyle, Aimee Einstein, Rich Elderkin, Melissa Eng, Bethany Goad, Beth Kerr, Ben Kou, Niki

The How and Why: Taking Care of Business With The Enneagram

Marutsos, Camille Naea, Ingrid Orellana, Elizabeth Perusse, Sam Roberts, Corrine Root, Nicky Rowe, Ellen Schecter, Jesset Sidore, Lesa Valentine, my "buddy" Pam Waddington, Danielle Weksler (whose intuitive, creative, and expert team coaching inspired an additional exercise in Chapter 11), and Fontane Yeung, all of whom have embraced the system and encouraged its use for the betterment of the organizations in which we work(ed) together. Additionally, Drs. Barbara Belk and Scott Hartvigsen, Dr. Robin Luke and Art Birakos, Bruce Carpenter, Brian Couch, Patricia DeLorenzi, Bud Dillon and Rudy Guerrero, Steve Garber and Bill Bonnet, Emmett Koehler, Linda Konopka, Janet Konopka-Fallon and Greg Fallon, Darren Main, Andrew Marsh and Robbie Frederick and Cha Cha and Ziggy and Turbo, Jeff McCoy, Ava Newman, Tom Sloan, and Richard Trilles have all been with me during this great journey of continuous learning, discovery, and deepening of understanding.

This work contains elements of my 25+ years of Human Resources and Organization Development experience in and exposure to myriad organizations and industries, sprinkled with Enneagram theory and practical applications of OD principles and interventions. It is not meant to be an end state and cure-all to all organizational vices and challenges. There is no such thing. Nor is it meant to represent the ultimate in knowledge in this ever-evolving field. It is meant as an aggregation and integration of the great work and thought that is happening around the globe to advance insight and understanding in ourselves and our organizations, with the intent of making things (at least slightly) better. Right now, we are all doing the best we can with what knowledge and tools we have amassed. Developing and adopting innovative perspectives and ways of looking at things is imperative in meeting and resolving today's business challenges. Maya Angelou is quoted saying, "Do the best you can until you know better. When you know better, do better." I am certain that we will know and do even more and better in the future. This is just another step in our never-ending progress and development. And as Russ Hudson stated at the 2016 International Enneagram Association Global Conference in Minneapolis, Minnesota, "it's an evolving field with no finish line."

And speaking of evolution, I am beyond thrilled to present the Second Edition of *The How and Why: Taking Care of Business with the Enneagram*. This 2021 version contains the following content enhancements from the original edition, released in 2016:

- Insertion of the Eisenhower/Covey "Urgent/Important Matrix" in Chapter 5, to assist in using values and other "True North" criteria in prioritization
- Connection of trust and empowerment to Decision-Making, Problem-Solving, and Innovation in Chapter 7, including the updating of the existing rubric and its practical application
- Expansion of Chapter 10 to include the connection between the Enneagram and Leadership Circle frameworks, enabling practitioners who use both to

leverage the insights of the Enneagram in optimizing their coachees'/clients' development
- Inclusion of an additional exercise in Chapter 11, designed to increase team cohesion and trust-building, and addition of a team take-away
- Incorporation of coaching questions to drive accountability in Chapter 13
- Enrichment of Chapter 14 with a recommended process flow to address conflict resolution via the Harmonic triads
- Incorporation of Galbraith's Star Model of Organization Design in Chapter 15, explained through the lens of the Process Enneagram
- Addition of a chapter on the Enneagram in Agility (Chapter 16), showing how the principles of the Enneagram play out in the tenets of agility
- Addition of Appendix F, a reference/reminder for facilitators to optimize their effectiveness and success by accessing, channeling, and leveraging all the energies of the Enneagram
- Updated "References and Additional Resources" section, including new relevant resources published since 2016

Chapter 1

Sense-Making

People go through life trying to make sense of the world around them. We wonder why some people misunderstand us, while we feel more in sync with others. Many of these differences have been explained or excused as cultural variations, personality preferences, and motivational dynamics. But the common denominator when we're trying to get anything done successfully – whether it's communicating, influencing, building a team, implementing a project plan, managing a change effort, creating a strategic plan, or trying to assure that everyone will be delighted (or at least not offended) at our next event – is the ability to take on another person's point of view. This is commonly referred to as "walking a mile in someone else's shoes" or empathy. It all comes down to our ability to let go of our belief that our perspective (and resultant opinion) is the right and only one and to reject the natural inclination to try to get everyone to do things our way. That line of thinking can come in handy in certain situations, but a more effective route is to open ourselves up to other ways of thinking. We cannot afford to be arrogant and self-centered. Groupthink is the most severe and extreme manifestation of this myopic phenomenon – and it can result in devastating consequences, like 1986's *Challenger* space shuttle disaster. On the opposite end of the spectrum, being open to and considering other perspectives can result in reaping enormous benefits from leveraging diversity, nurturing innovation, and optimizing problem-solving.

In our quest to find meaning and make sense of the world, application of situationally-appropriate models can be useful. My life path has introduced me to the Enneagram and I find the components of its framework to be particularly applicable to many situations. Heeding my own advice, I am not advocating that the Enneagram is the "be all and end all" of all models, or that everything else is irrelevant. On the contrary, I advise using complementary instruments to gain a better and more comprehensive understanding of the world around us. However, in the absence of researching, learning, and staying on top of every new model, system, framework, and flavor of the month, there is great value and efficiency in understanding the intricacies of one system and seeing how it can be applied to solve a multitude of organizational challenges.

As such, I have attempted to identify the best practices and most-used models in the field of Organization Development, and find out how the additional insights of the Enneagram model can be used as an overlay or enhancement to make them even more powerful and effective. My corporate roles in Learning and Organization Development have served me well in encountering and using myriad tools, theories, and frameworks. These are all intended to help managers and leaders gain greater clarity and understanding around how to optimize performance from their people and achieve as much output as possible to meet ever-increasing targets and goals. Many of these happen to take the form of simplistic two-by-two grids (i.e., Jack Welch's 4 Box model of performance, the Johari Window, the Blanchard or Hersey Situational Leadership Models, DiSC, the Eisenhower or Covey Urgent/Important Matrix). Notice a trend? They are all easily-digestible and accessible tactical solutions to the many universal challenges that organizations have faced when dealing with the human element. They nicely, neatly, and clearly address, treat, and serve as band aids for the cuts and bruises encountered in the course of normal, day-to-day business operations. And, as such, they are barely scratching the surface of what deeper issues are really causing some of these symptoms.

Sometimes / It Depends

Just as Hersey and Blanchard discuss adopting and implementing different leadership styles that align to the situation presented, I want to caution practitioners to not fall into the trap that, when we have a hammer, we start interpreting every challenge we encounter as a nail. It is important to round out our toolkits so that we can choose the most appropriate tool to use in the different situations and environments we encounter. If there is one thing that the study of psychology (even organizational psychology) teaches us, it is that there rarely exists a single appropriate and predictable answer to a problem. Since there is no single, right solution, we usually need to collect more information, especially about the context, and specifically to identify the real cause, not just treat its symptoms. And that is why a perfectly acceptable answer to most organizational dilemmas and challenges is "It depends." Or "sometimes." We will always be right when responding with either of these two answers. To avoid being perceived as overly glib, we must then follow up with the explanation of the appropriate circumstance where the proposed solution will work, with respect and acknowledgement, of course, to the specific situation at hand. This tactic is also intended to prevent viewing every situation as a nail to be fixed by our exclusive hammer, be it the Enneagram or any other model. Having a repertoire of tools, models, and frameworks from which to choose will broaden the robustness of our options, solutions, and likelihood of success.

How to Use this Resource

Consider this to be an overview of Organization Development tools and frameworks traditionally associated with solving typical business challenges, infused and enhanced with the Enneagram – a bridge or foundation of insight. It is not meant to be prescriptive or exhaustive. It is intended to manifest the alignment between the Enneagram model and currently-used solutions, and inspire practitioners to discuss and create their own hybrid approaches to organizational challenges being presented to them. Complementary use of the Enneagram with these models, or integrating its insights in these situations, can help create more robust and effective solutions. Different people will have different experiences with, opinions and understanding of, and comfort level with each of these frameworks. It is, of course, always up to the practitioner to decide the best tool with which to address each unique situation, based on an in-depth intake consultation. Each of the following chapters provides some options for your consideration.

Chapter 2

Introducing the Enneagram into Business Settings

The following is a sample process Human Resources and Organization Development practitioners can use to introduce the Enneagram to teams of businesspeople in corporate settings during a workshop.

The saying "Knowing yourself is the beginning of all wisdom" has been credited to both Aristotle and Socrates. Although we will never know which one of these famous Greek philosophers actually uttered these words, we can use this concept to help guide self-awareness and development. The Johari Window is an excellent place to build our foundation in understanding that our self-perceptions may not necessarily align with what others see, experience, and, consequently, think of us. This is our first clue that we need to increase our self-awareness, a precursor to developing our emotional intelligence. The model calls out that there are many different facets of ourselves, which we may choose to divulge or conceal, assuming we are cognizant of them, and that other people may see things that we don't yet recognize about ourselves. It even allows for unknown territory about which we and others may be unaware.

	KNOWN TO SELF	NOT KNOWN TO SELF
KNOWN TO OTHERS	Open	Blind Spot
NOT KNOWN TO OTHERS	Hidden	Unknown

Figure 2-1 | The Johari Window

Once we become aware of the potential gaps between how we see ourselves and how others experience us, we can then start the personal work necessary to develop any areas that are inconsistent with how we want to be and be seen. The action of "opening up" the Johari Window and ourselves to others helps us to build trust and relationships with them. And brings us to the next important step: debunking a popular standard rule.

Throughout our lives, we have all been taught the importance and pervasiveness of the Golden Rule. Many variations of this exist, including:
- Do unto others as you would have them do unto you
- Treat others the way you want to be treated
- S/he who has the gold, rules (Ok, this last one may be a little tongue-in-cheek, but still true, no?)

While I don't dispute the general and overall value of living one's life according to this principle, there is another school of thought that challenges the devotees of this somewhat myopic mantra to widen their horizons and consider adopting the Platinum Rule: "Treat others the way *they* want to be treated." Once we have taken this leap from a *self-focused* approach of interacting with others (which requires us to understand how we like to be treated) to an *other-focused* approach (which requires us to find out how *others* want to be treated), we are inherently increasing our emotional intelligence. We accomplish this by understanding and accepting that there may, indeed, be a difference between these two states.

How many times have we encountered a situation where we immediately defaulted to what is easy and familiar to us? And out of those situations, how often have we been successful in evaluating and responding to the situation appropriately? And how often have we considered changing our methods to achieve the desired result? Here, it might behoove us to remind ourselves about the definition of insanity: Doing the same thing over and over again and expecting different results. Let's try something new instead. Let's widen our repertoire to include some new tricks and tools to help us achieve our goals and, in the process, gain a greater understanding of ourselves, our coworkers, our stakeholders, and our interpersonal dynamics.

Consider this exercise to drive the point home. Poll the workshop participants to see if anyone already knows or has heard of the Enneagram. Find out what they already know. Most will not have heard of it. Some may make a connection to Myers-Briggs. Briefly describe the Enneagram as a personality/motivation/development framework, attributed to and based on the teachings of Russia's George Ivanovitch Gurdjieff, Bolivia's Oscar Ichazo, and Chile's Claudio Naranjo. It has become more widely used in organizations since its more widespread dissemination in the San Francisco Bay Area started in the 1970s.

Tell them that they may not realize it, but they actually all already know the Enneagram and will teach it to each other during the workshop. Reassure them that the goal here is not to try to type or box anyone, but rather to understand that each of us has a different, default focus of attention.

To provide greater understanding about the role of "default operating systems," ask the workshop participants to each take out a blank piece of paper and sign their name on it. Now ask them to switch hands and repeat the task. (Alternatively, this exercise can also be conducted without paper, by asking them to cross their arms in front of themselves and then asking them to cross their arms the opposite way). Debrief the exercise by asking:

"How did it feel the first time you signed your name (or crossed your arms)?" Typical answers will include:
- Natural
- Muscle memory
- Easy
- Didn't think about it at all
- Fast

Then ask how it felt the second time. Likely responses will include:
- Illegible
- Hard

The How and Why: Taking Care of Business With The Enneagram

- Took longer
- Had to concentrate more and exert more effort

Now explain the point of the exercise: "As human beings, we all have default ways of thinking and doing things that we have developed, honed, and strengthened throughout our lives. These have now become second nature to us because of our comfort in doing them. This doesn't mean we can't do things in other ways – it just means that when we do things differently, it may take longer and not be as elegant or pretty. But if we repeatedly practice the new skill or behavior, it, too, can become very natural and more easily accessible. And it will make us more effective in situations that may call for this new perspective, behavior, and skill."

Now that they have a better understanding of default operating systems, it's time to facilitate their learning and teaching each other the Enneagram. Take a flipchart sheet of paper (or use a dry erase whiteboard) and draw a circle in the middle of it. Add in the Enneagram Type numbers (1 through 9) in their appropriate locations around the circle and ask the group "What motivates people?" Or, alternatively, "What inspires people?" Or, "What do people really find important?" Or, "What gets people out of bed in the morning?" Repeat this question (or one or more of its variants) to yield a robust and meaningful list of values that can be easily placed within and assigned to the overall categories identified in the Enneagram system.

As the workshop participants call out their answers, plot them around the circle, placing each one next to the

Enneagram Type with which it is most aligned. When answers come up that could relate to more than one type (i.e., "recognition" can be affiliated with Enneatypes 2 and/or 3 and/or 4; "challenge" may be related to Enneatypes 3 and 8), plot them in all places and/or tease out the real underlying motivation by asking, "Recognition for what?" This will help the group see that different people want to be recognized for different reasons (and that there are different types of recognition). Sometimes, some very interesting answers may arise from frustrated aspiring comedians, such as "Sex" or "Beer." Have fun with these and put them at point 7. Pretending to mis-hear "fear" as "beer" can also add some levity and humor to the exercise!

Indubitably, when working in corporate, for-profit environments, some of the first responses will revolve around money, bonuses, challenges, and other rewards and recognition for meeting and/or exceeding performance goals. And that is the generally accepted and used model in US organizations. But it's not the full story. Keep asking the group that same question and keep brainstorming answers. At the end of ten minutes, a relatively long list will be revealed, including some of these possibilities:

- Ethics
- Beliefs (including Spiritual/Religious)
- Values
- Goals
- Challenges
- Fear

The How and Why: Taking Care of Business With The Enneagram

- Comfort
- Achievement
- Recognition
- Fun
- Adventure
- Relationships
- Family
- Helping others
- Continuous learning
- Knowledge
- Power
- Control
- Authority

Given enough time and gentle prodding, these more elusive answers may also emerge:

- Collaborating with others; Collaborative work environment
- Being unique/special; Doing unique/special work
- Purpose, meaning

It is common for it to take a relatively long period of time to tease out the values associated with Enneagram types 1, 4, and 9, especially in for-profit organization audiences. Play with it. Explain that some values are more readily associated with for-profit organizations and that Enneatypes 1, 4, and 9 may be more attracted to working in non-profit organizations.

Generally, a diagram that resembles the one that follows will be produced each time:

Figure 2-2 | What Motivates People?

The groundwork is now laid to help explain the Enneagram framework to businesspeople. Once people are given the opportunity to come up with these answers on their own, the point is driven home: there is more than one way to motivate people. Different people are, indeed, motivated by different factors. Plus, having the workshop participants come up with the answers is more empowering and engaging to them (some even see it as a competitive game to have words at each point) and more meaningful than the facilitator simply droning on. Furthermore, this methodology helps to diminish any resistance from skeptics, since they and their teammates are the ones coming up with the content!

The next step is to walk around the circle, explaining each type by name(s), the best way to motivate and demotivate each type, and the strengths that each type brings to the workplace. This latter part is meant to combat criticism that traditional Enneagram models tend to focus too much on the negative aspects of each type.

This will, inevitably, generate many epiphanies from workshop attendees, who will, just due to their human nature, start identifying people in their home and work lives who exemplify these characteristics. It is obviously valuable to understand the Enneagram types of one's direct reports, peers, customers, bosses, and other stakeholders in order to motivate and reward them appropriately, communicate and present to them according to what they consider to be important, and not inadvertently – or advertently! – push their hot buttons. However, there is no way for us to know for sure another person's Enneagram type simply based on his/her observable behavior.

At this point, it is necessary to quell this natural human response and advise them of the danger of "typing" other people. Despite the fact that people may behave in a certain

ENNEATYPE	MOTIVATORS	DEMOTIVATORS	VALUE-ADD TO TEAM
1 Perfectionist / Reformer	Doing the right thing, ethics, values, morals	Unethical/immoral leadership, inequality, unfairness	Discernment: Focus on finding out whats wrong and fixing/improving it; being the moral compass
2 Helper / Giver	Connections, relationships, being needed	Feeling unneeded or unappreciated for their contributions/support	Helpfulness, seeing what's needed and fulfilling the need
3 Performer / Achiever	Goals, achievement, money, recognition	Blocking their ability to reach their goal, harming their reputation or image of being the best at ___	Focus on goals, efficiency, getting things done, action oriented
4 Romantic / Artist	Authenticity, beauty, being special, originality uniqueness	Feeling common, ordinary, "run-of-the-mill"	Creativity, identifying what's missing, empathetic connection to feelings and emotions of others
5 Observer / Analyst	Wisdom, knowledge, learning, information, data	Forced connection to people, change	Analysis, objectivity
6 Loyal Skeptic	Comfort, security, safety	Threats to personal safety, comfort, security	Contingency/ worst case scenario planning
7 Adventurer / Epicure	Fun, opportunities, options, experiences	Limits, constraints	Ideas, innovation, fun, excitement, spirit
8 Boss / Protector	Power, control, authority, truth, justice	Injustice, threat to their turf, mistreatment of their people	Execution, action orientation, driving accountability, protecting team
9 Mediator / Peacekeeper	Harmonious, collaborative, positive environments	Change to the status quo, conflict	Collaboration, seeing all perspectives

Figure 2-3 | Motivators, Demotivators, and Team Value-Add by Enneagram Type

way, we have no way of really knowing the reason *why* they do so, as we can't read their minds. By predicting or guessing other people's Enneagram types, we are falling under the seductive spell of the fundamental attribution error/bias, whereby we interpret their behavior according to our limited and self-referencing personal history and viewpoint rather than truly understanding theirs. Remind them of the ethics of any self-assessment/personality typing system:

- The only person who is qualified to assess, accept, reveal, and publicize his/her type is the person him/herself. It's fair to say that most of us are not mind-readers, so we don't know what is going on in people's heads and we can't readily identify their motivations. Because we don't fully know anyone, we also don't know their backgrounds, level of integration, mental health, histories, influences, or traumas that can contribute to their behaviors and mask their true motivations. There are also many factors (such as parental overlays, strong wing associations, and subtypes) that can make some types look and act like other types. For these reasons, we should not guess or share another person's type, especially without their permission. And especially not over social media.
- Each type is equally valuable and has unique gifts and strengths. Of course, overuse or overreliance on these comfortable defaults can lead to them becoming weaknesses that can derail one's career and relationships. There is no one type that is better than any other type. We need representation of all types in order to gain a full and robust perspective and understanding of the world.

Otherwise, we only access and experience a 40 degree limited sliver of it. In addition, to counter the argument that the Enneagram (or any other classification system) puts people into boxes opening them up to judgment by others, remember that we are all combinations of all the types – we may have a built-in default mode, and some types may be more readily accessible to us than others, but we always have the capability to select which way to interpret and react to a stimulus.

- It is, at minimum, unethical (and hopefully someday, illegal) to make employment decisions based on an assumption or revelation of someone's type. This question should never come up in an interview as it has no work-related legal bearing. Any person of any type can be successful in any job to which s/he aspires and for which s/he has developed the necessary skills and competencies. Aspiration and interest/passion always trump an archetypical personality type that may lack aspiration/interest in the work.
- People aren't their type. They "do," affiliate/lead with, or channel a type's motivations, perspectives, and characteristics. And this may be their primary, "default operating system" type or any other type they may choose. This explanation can help placate the fears of those who are concerned about being "put in a box," stereotyped, or pre-judged by others as a result of revealing their primary type.
- As with any self-assessment instrument, we must rely

on the person's self-awareness level for an accurate report. It sometimes takes people years to correctly "type" themselves. Sitting with a panel or group of their own Enneagram type sometimes helps people identify their own type; they tend to feel a kinship and a "homecoming" in the presence of kindred spirits. Great progress continues to be made in the arena of highly-validated and reliable assessment instruments that can assist people in their journey of finding their probable type (i.e., see Integrative Enneagram Solutions).

- Each framework is designed and intended to be helpful and contribute to self-development and self-improvement. It is not to be used for evil purposes, such as manipulating others. We can use these to increase our emotional intelligence. This consists of becoming more self-aware about our own motivations, preferences, perspectives, and ideologies and how they impact our interactions with others. The second component of emotional intelligence is to improve our understanding of others' motivations, preferences, perspectives, and ideologies – and how they may differ from our own. Upon increasing our ability to empathize with others, the ultimate step of emotional intelligence is to alter our own behaviors and actions to match the situation presented to us and optimize the chances of a successful interaction and outcome.

Remind them, too, that this exercise simply serves as an introduction to the system. The purpose is to reveal the nine different primary motivators for people and to consider that others are probably motivated by factors different from one's own (recall the Platinum Rule). To underscore this point, especially with Enneagram novices who may not already know their default Enneagram type, ask them to select the top three types that resonate with them based on the limited descriptions provided in the exercise (or hand out the chart in Appendix A: "You Know You're Accessing Enneagram Type _ If/When …"). Explain that sometimes people tend to affiliate with a different type from each of the Head (Enneatypes 5, 6, and 7), Heart (Enneatypes 2, 3, and 4), or Gut (Enneatypes 8, 9, and 1) Triads – and that this is the way in which they tend to access their thinking, feeling, and actions, respectively. Ask the team for each individual to raise his/her hand when one of the Enneatypes is called out that matches their top three affiliations. Inform the group that it's okay to look around the room to see who raises his/her hand for the different choices. That drives the point home that different people are motivated by different factors and experience the world differently.

Most people will experience flashbacks to "Maslow" and "Hierarchy of Needs" when the subject of motivation comes up. Feel free to remind them of these important motivators, while interjecting some humor. Re-introduce Maslow's Hierarchy of Needs, as amended and updated to reflect modern sensibilities:

The How and Why: Taking Care of Business With The Enneagram

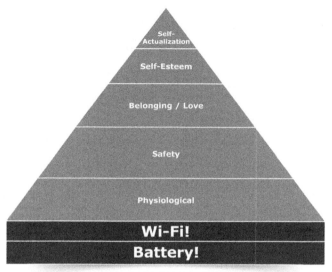

Figure 2-4 | Maslow Revisited

Looking at Maslow's theory and its possible integration or alignment with other popular systems of human motivation, we can surmise that only after basic human needs for survival are met do we see other factors gain importance. That means that, in our capitalistic and commercial society, once enough money on which to survive (or sustain a lifestyle to which one aspires) is no longer a consideration, the interplay between other researchers' findings will become more significant for individuals. Let's see how we can make sense of these complementary systems:

Maslow's framework aligns neatly with the primary needs and motivations of individuals identified in the Enneagram:
- Physiological (food, water, shelter, warmth) and Safety (security, stability, freedom from fear) needs can be easily aligned to Enneatype 6 needs for safety and security

and the Self-Preservation subtype. Enneatype 8 may also fit into this category as it spills over into the next higher order need due to their strength at controlling their environment while protecting and caring for their close inner circle.
- The need for belonging (friends, family, spouse, lover) and to be loved is directly connected to the people-pleasing Enneatypes 2 and 9.
- Self-esteem needs (related to achievement, mastery, recognition, and respect) are the focus of the Competency Triad comprised of Enneatypes 1, 3, and 5.
- The elusive Self-Actualization need (pursuit of inner talent, creativity, and fulfillment) are lifelong pursuits of Enneatypes 4 and, possibly, Enneatype 7.

Dan Pink's model of motivation calls out universal employee needs for autonomy (7), mastery (the Competency Triad of Enneatypes 1, 3, 5), and purpose (4), while Adam Grant focuses on fairness (1), safety (6), and control (8). Combined together, we can see that these two perspectives almost complete the nine Enneagram style needs and areas of focus, although, in this scenario, Enneatypes 2 and 9 seem to be missing. To paraphrase Tina "What's love got to do with it?" Turner, who needs relationships and harmony anyway? Recall that it is not surprising that Enneatype 9 is absent from the synthesis of these complementary frameworks, since the qualities associated with Enneatypes 9, 1, and 4 are usually the last to be unearthed, or are even never discovered, in the "What motivates people?" exercise, as discussed earlier.

Showing managers and leaders the relationship between these seminal motivation theories and modern adaptations can give them a better understanding of the Enneagram and see how it fits into and relates to these schemas. It can also serve as a great reminder that there are additional motivational factors to consider that may not be included in some current models.

Chapter 3

Recruitment, Engagement, and Retention

So how does this play out in the workplace? In 2007, I set out to answer just that by testing my hypothesis that people tend to join, stay with, and leave organizations based on met/unmet needs related to their Enneagram types. Specifically, I discovered statistically significant support that:

- Those who affiliated with Enneatype 1 valued supervisory integrity more than Enneatypes 4 and 8 when deciding to join past organizations. They also differed from Enneatypes 3 and 4 in using that dimension when choosing to stay with their current company. Additionally, Enneatype 1s differed from Enneatype 3s in valuing the aggregate literature review–based factors more when choosing to stay with their current employers.
- Those who affiliated with Enneatype 6 differed from Enneatype 4s in their higher valuation of trust in leadership as a factor in deciding to join an organization (as did Enneatypes 1, 5, 7, and 9).
- A collaborative work environment was more important for those who affiliated with Enneatype 9 than

Enneatype 4 in their decisions to remain with past employers.
- Sufficient time off was valued more by those who affiliated with Enneatypes 5 and 6 than Enneatype 3s in choosing to stay with past employers. Those who affiliated with Enneatypes 6, 1, and 2 valued trust in leadership more than Enneatype 4s in their decisions to remain in past organizations.
- Further analysis by subtype revealed statistically significant differences between Social and Sexual/1:1 counterparts in the former's higher valuation of innovative work when having chosen to join and remain with past organizations. Social subtypes differed from Self-Preservation peers when having chosen to stay with a past employer based on a collaborative work environment. Sexual/1:1 subtypes differed from Social subtypes in their valuation of supervisory support when having decided to stay with past employers, and from both other subtypes when factoring in interesting work.

The variables identified in my literature review were:
- Career development (encompassing mentoring, training and development, and career growth opportunities)
- Challenging/meaningful work that is related to an employee's career interests
- Employer culture and reputation
- Organizational commitment/job involvement/recognition

- Support from one's organization/supervisor
- Honest and truthful recruitment processes (e.g., Realistic Job Previews)
- Competitive, individually-based compensation and benefits

DECISION POINT	FACTOR / VARIABLE	MORE IMPORTANT FOR	LESS IMPORTANT FOR	HYPOTHESIS
Attraction	Supervisor's Integrity	1	8,4	Yes, 1
Attraction	Trust in Leadership	1,5,6,7,9	4	Yes, 6
Attraction	Fair / Just Use of Power	1	4	No
Attraction	Collaborative Work Environment	9	4	Yes, 9
Retention (Past)	Supervisor's Integrity	1	4,3	Yes, 1
Retention (Past)	Sufficient Time Off	6,5	3	Yes, 5
Retention (Past)	Trust in Leadership	6,1,2	4	Yes, 6
Retention (Past)	Literature Review Variables	1	3	Yes
Retention (Current)	Competitive Skill-Based Pay	1	3	Literature Review
Attraction	Innovative Work	Social	1:1	N/A
Retention (Past)	Innovative Work	Social	1:1	N/A
Retention (Past)	Collaborative Work Environment	Social	Self-Preservation	N/A
Retention (Past)	Supervisory Support	1:1	Social	N/A
Retention (Past)	Interesting Work	1:1	Social Self-Preservation	N/A

Figure 3-1 | Enneagram-Related Employment Decision Factors, $P<0.05$

The How and Why: Taking Care of Business With The Enneagram

DECISION POINT	FACTOR / VARIABLE	MORE IMPORTANT FOR	LESS IMPORTANT FOR	HYPOTHESIS
Attraction	Supervisor's Support	1,6,2,3,5,9	7,4,8	Yes, 2
Attraction	Competitive, Skills-Based Pay	5,1,9,6,2	4,8,3,7	No
Attraction	Job Security	1,2	9,6,5,7,4,8,3	No
Attraction	Job Involvement/ Connect to work	All	None	Literature Review
Retention (Past)	Employer Culture/ Values	All	None	Literature Review
Retention (Past)	Feeling Appreciated	6,2,1,7,9,4,5,8	3	Yes, 2
Retention (Past)	Career Development Opportunities	1,7,6,9,5,8,2	4,3	Literature Review
Retention (Past)	Employer Reputation/ Values	1,6,7,2,9,8	4,5,3	Literature Review
Retention (Past)	Honest and Truthful Recruitment	8,6	7,5,2,4,9,1,3	Literature Review
Retention (Past)	Fair and Just Use of Power	6,1,5,8,2,9,7	4,3	Yes, 8
Retention (Past)	Collaborative Work Environment	9,6,1,7,3,2,5,8	4	Yes, 9
Retention (Current)	Employer Reputation/ Values	1,6,2,9,8,7	4,5,3	Literature Review

Figure 3-2 | Enneagram-Related Employment Decision Factors, $0.05 < P < 0.08$

For the more data- and detail-focused readers of this book, here are the specifics:

Overarching Hypothesis: Respondents self-report a pattern of joining, staying with, and leaving organizations consistent with the factors identified in the retention literature review.

This hypothesis was partially supported. The results pertaining to this hypothesis showed a significant difference between Enneatype 1s' overall valuation of the literature review factors as compared to Enneatype 3s. Enneatype 1s valued the variables found in the literature review significantly more (5.1 versus 3.7) than Enneatype 3s in this sample. Therefore, it is shown that at least one Enneatype (Type 1) self-reports a pattern of staying with organizations based on the aggregate factors reported in the literature.

Hypothesis 1: Enneatype 1s self-report a pattern of joining, staying with, and leaving organizations based on their perception/experience of how ethical and reputable those organizations and their supervisors within them are.

This hypothesis was partially supported with regard to supervisor integrity. Note that the organization's reputation was not a significantly different factor for Enneatype 1s as compared to their counterparts, but that supervisor's integrity was, since the relationship with the supervisor is called out as an important variable in the literature review.

Nevertheless, significant differences were noted in Enneatype 1s decisions to join past organizations considering supervisor's integrity (as compared to Enneatypes 4 and 8), trust in leadership (along with Enneatypes 5, 6, 7, and 9 as compared to Enneatype 4s), and their valuation of fair and just use of power (versus Enneatypes 4s). Supervisory integrity was again an important factor with significant differences as compared to Enneatypes 4 and 3 when deciding to stay with an organization, as was trust in leadership (again) as compared to Enneatypes 3 and 4. Enneatype 1s also differed significantly from their Enneatype 3 counterparts in valuing competitive, skill-based pay in their decision to stay with their current employer (although this finding could be skewed based on the low sample size of Enneatype 3 respondents and the fact that most of them were retired). Although supervisory integrity was predicted as a factor for Enneatype 1s to select, the other findings are also not surprising. Trust in leadership, fair and just use of power, and competitive, skills-based pay are all factors relating to "doing the right thing" and equitable treatment, which would fall within the domain of Enneatype 1 values and morals. The statistically significant emphasis on trusting leadership in decisions to join past organizations by Enneatypes 5, 6, 7, and 9 (compared to Enneatype 4s) could be attributed to all of these Enneatypes' commonality at the Enneatype 6 — both Enneatypes 5 and 7 have a 6 wing and Enneatype 9s go to 6 under stress. A trustworthy leader would probably contribute to a work environment that would feel more safe and secure and allay this primary concern of Enneatype 6s. Furthermore, a trustworthy leader would probably be more likely to create a harmonious and fair environment, further appealing to these Enneatype 9 sensibilities. Keep in mind, too, that Enneatype 9s have a 1 wing which can also come into play to explain the emphasis on this Enneatype 1 quality, assuming leadership trustworthiness is related to supervisory integrity.

The consistency exhibited in the Enneatype 1 versus Enneatype 4 dichotomy is of particular interest, especially considering that the 4 is the stress type of Enneatype 1s and that the 1 is the security type of Enneatype 4s. This could imply that Enneatypes may have ideological conflict with Enneatypes of their stress arrow. More research needs to be conducted in this arena. This scenario also plays out with the Enneatype 6 versus Enneatype 3 dichotomy in "sufficient time off."

Hypothesis 2: Enneatype 2s self-report a pattern of joining, staying with, and leaving organizations based on their perception/experience of whether they are valued/needed/respected by those organizations.

This hypothesis was not supported. The only significant difference noted involving the Enneatype 2 compared to other Enneatype responses was for trust in leadership as a factor in staying with past employers. This was in comparison to Enneatype 4s. This may be explained by drawing upon the Enneatype 2s relationship-orientation and organizational tendency to support leaders (Palmer & Brown, 1997). The relationship-building with and support of leaders would imply a trust in that leadership. Otherwise, cognitive dissonance would occur. That trust in leadership could be a result of feeling valued and needed, which are all elements of the Enneatype 2 schema.

Hypothesis 3: Enneatype 3s self-report a pattern of joining, staying with, and leaving organizations based on their perception/experience of whether those organizations are able to provide them with the titles, positions, and rewards they seek.

This hypothesis was not supported. There were several significant differences noted for Type 3s, always compared to Enneatype 1, but none to support the hypothesis. In fact, the opposite was shown with the significant difference noted between Enneatypes 1 and 3 in their valuation of competitive, skills-based pay factoring into their decisions to stay with their current employers. This could be explained by the fact that the Enneatype 3s were underrepresented in this sample and 3 of the 5 respondents were retired, while another respondent earned over $200,000 a year. These factors may have skewed the results since compensation may have not been a factor for these respondents at the time they took the survey; that may have clouded their judgment of past employment situations. Another explanation could be the wording of the question: "competitive, skills-based pay." This may not be a motivating factor to Enneatype 3s, who might be seeking remuneration in excess of that. The significant differences between Enneatype 1s and 3s call for additional research to study whether there are conflicts or consistent differences in other areas between the steadfast, values-driven Enneatype 1s and the chameleon-like, results-driven Enneatype 3s.

Hypothesis 4: Enneatype 4s self-report a pattern of joining, staying with, and leaving organizations based on their perception/experience of the uniqueness and innovation of their work within those organizations.

This hypothesis was not supported. As with the Enneatype 3s, there were several significant differences noted for

Enneatype 4s, although none supported the hypothesis. Enneatype 4s exhibited the most significant differences as compared to the other Enneatypes, but on a negative scale. This means that the factors presented mattered less to them than the other Enneatypes, specifically the Enneatypes 1, 2, 6, and 9. This difference in value structure hints at the unique nature of the Enneatype 4s and may contribute to their feeling different from others. This is the only respondent group that differed significantly against so many other different Enneatype groups. Note that, in comparison to their other Enneatype counterparts, Enneatype 4s were more likely to have worked for 6 or more industries during their 25+ year careers (68% of respondents have worked for more than 25 years). One third of Enneatype 4 respondents reported this, whereas 75% of all the other types reported that their careers spanned 5 or fewer industries. This anomaly may be attributed to Enneatype 4's longing for something different, which manifests itself in changes in the type of industry in which they work in an attempt to achieve this.

Hypothesis 5: Enneatype 5s self-report a pattern of joining, staying with, and leaving organizations based on their perception/experience of whether personal privacy, time off, and educational opportunities exist for them within those organizations.

This hypothesis was partially supported. "Sufficient time off" was selected as a factor that would be of probable importance to Enneatype 5s, perhaps due to their reserved nature and affinity for educational pursuits. As predicted, Enneatype 5s differed significantly from Enneatype 3s in this regard, valuing their time away from work more highly than their stereotypically workaholic counterparts, when deciding to stay with past employers.

Hypothesis 6: Enneatype 6s self-report a pattern of joining, staying with, and leaving organizations based on their perception/experience of whether their jobs are secure within those organizations and their level of trust in their supervisors and/or leaders.

This hypothesis was supported. Enneatype 6s differed significantly from Enneatype 4s in both deciding to join and stay with past employers on their evaluation of their organization's leadership. There was also a difference noted in their higher valuation of paid time off of work versus their Enneatype 3 counterparts, which was not predicted. Perhaps this could be attributed to the Enneatype 6 respondents' exhibition of a strong 5 wing tendency; the hypothesis related to this was supported. As discussed in the Enneatype 1 section, this could also be evidence of discord with one's stressor, where the Enneatype 6s differ from their Enneatype 3 stress point.

Hypothesis 7: Enneatype 7s self-report a pattern of joining, staying with, and leaving organizations based on their perception/experience of whether fun and variety are available for them in those organizations, especially manifest in innovative and interesting work.

This hypothesis was not supported. The only significant difference involving Enneatype 7s was in comparison to the Enneatype 4s, in the former's higher valuation of trust in leadership in joining an organization. In the hypotheses, this factor was selected for Enneatype 6s, potentially due to their skeptical nature. This finding could be attributed to Enneatype 7s with strong 6 wings factoring into their decision-making process.

Hypothesis 8: Enneatype 8s self-report a pattern of joining, staying with, and leaving organizations based on their perception/experience of the extent of autonomy and control they have in their positions within those organizations and whether there is fairness and justice in the use of power in those organizations.

This hypothesis was not supported. The only significant difference involving Enneatype 8s was found in comparison to Enneatype 1s in the former's lower emphasis on supervisory integrity as a factor in deciding to join past organizations.

Hypothesis 9: Enneatype 9s self-report a pattern of joining, staying with, and leaving organizations based on their perception/experience of whether their work/role/goals are clearly and well-defined within those organization and/or their experience of a collaborative work environment.

This hypothesis was partially supported. Traditionally harmony-seeking Enneatype 9s differed significantly from

Enneatype 4s in their higher valuation of a collaborative work environment when deciding to join an organization. This difference could be attributed to Enneatype 4s feeling unique and that their special contributions are more individually-oriented than team-focused. This would have to be studied further for validation. Enneatype 9s also manifested a significant difference from their Enneatype 4 counterparts in their decision to join organizations based on their valuation of trustworthiness of leadership (which could contribute to a collaborative work environment). Note that the significant differences were only found for Enneatype 9s seeking a collaborative working environment when joining an organization and that a collaborative working environment was not found to be a statistically significantly different factor for Enneatype 9s deciding to stay with or leave a company. This could be due to the purported tendency of Enneatype 9s in "going with the flow" and seeking to create harmony in whichever situation they find themselves. This quality would then help explain why Enneatype 9s may try to make the best of a situation that may not be as collaborative as they had initially hoped. Enneatype 9s were the only ones of the survey respondents whose careers consisted of working in just one company, for more than 15 years each. Or, Enneatype 9s may have made a correct up-front evaluation of their prospective work environments when deciding to join the organization that proved to meet their expectations of collaboration; thus, this may not be an issue in their potential decision to leave the environment. Further research needs to be conducted to verify these suppositions. In short:

TYPE	RULES OF ENGAGEMENT & MOTIVATION
1	• Follow the established rules, laws, policies, and processes. • Attract them with job security, supportive supervisors with integrity, and trustworthy leaders who use their power justly and fairly. • Retain them with competitive, skill-based pay, career development, and a reputable organization with whose values they resonate.
2	• Appreciate their contributions and help. • Include/involve them. • Attract them with supervisory support, competitive, skill-based pay, and job security. • Retain them with trustworthy leaders who use their power justly and fairly, making them feel appreciated, provide career development opportunities, and a collaborative, reputable organization with whose values they resonate.
3	• Attract them with a supportive supervisor. • Retain them with a collaborative work environment.
4	• Recognize and leverage their unique talents and artistry. • Retain them by making me feel appreciated.
5	• Give them their space and autonomy. • Attract them with trustworthy leadership, supportive leadership, and competitive, skill-based pay. • Retain them with sufficient time off, making them feel appreciated, provide career development, fair/just use of power, and a collaborative work environment.
6	• Make them feel safe, reassured, and comfortable. • Attract them with trustworthy, supportive leadership, and competitive, skill-based pay. • Retain them with sufficient time off, making them feel appreciated, provide career development, a reputable employer with whose values they align, honest/truthful recruitment, fair/just use of power, and a collaborative work environment.
7	• Give them lots of fun options. • Attract them with trustworthy leadership. • Retain them by making them feel appreciated, provide career development opportunities, ensure alignment with employer reputation and values, fair/just use of power, and a collaborative work environment.
8	• Challenge them; follow their lead. • Retain them by making them feel appreciated, with career development opportunities, honest and truthful recruitment, fair/just use of power, alignment with employer reputation/values, and a collaborative work environment.
9	• Give them direction. • Tell them what is expected of them. • Attract them with trustworthy leadership, a collaborative work environment, supportive leadership, and competitive, skill-based pay. • Retain them by making them feel appreciated, with career development, fair/just use of power, a collaborative work environment, and a reputable employment environment with whose values they align.

Figure 3-3 | Rules of Engagement by Enneagram Type

The How and Why: Taking Care of Business With The Enneagram

Now that managers have gained new awareness that individuals of varying Enneagram types respond to different motivating factors and environments, how can they use this knowledge to best support and motivate their team members if they don't know those team members' styles and can't accurately guess them?

Of course, opening the channels of communication with their direct reports is the easiest, most direct, and most effective tactic that managers can use to identify what employees want and need out of the working relationship. This can be accomplished through the use of a tool called a Stay Interview, which is the polar opposite of an Exit Interview. Finding out what didn't work for departing employees during an Exit Interview is usually too late to do anything about rectifying the issue(s). Furthermore, politically-savvy employees, who don't want to burn bridges, may not always reveal the truth during this process, or even participate in it at all. Enter the Stay Interview as a possible solution. During one-on-one sessions several times a year, managers are encouraged to ask their direct reports some pointed questions designed to uncover what management can do to make employees' work environments as ideal as possible, within appropriate business parameters, of course. These questions may yield some interesting data that managers can use to appropriately motivate their employees to stay with the organization (assuming, of course, they want them to!):

- What do you like about your work?
- What keeps you here?

- What makes for a great day at work?
- What is something new you would like to learn/do this year?
- What would you like to change about your job?
- What would you like to change about the team/department?
- How can we utilize your talents more fully?
- Which one thing could make your job more satisfying/rewarding?
- How can you feel better-supported in your career goals?
- How can you be better-recognized? For what?
- What kind of recognition is meaningful to you? Public? Private? Monetary? Other?
- When we frustrate each other or come into conflict with one another, how shall we best resolve it?

Managers may choose to delve deeper into any of the above questions to determine the reasoning behind their employees' answers by simply asking "Why?" several times until they get to the core motivation. This is not a one-time exercise; peoples' situations can and do change over the course of time. That makes revisiting this conversation necessary a few times a year in order to ascertain where an employee might be and what s/he might need at that point in time.

NOTE ON ETHICS

Despite what may be a fairly common interview practice, it may be illegal, unethical, and invalid to use a candidate's personality type (whether determined through Myers-Briggs Type Instrument, DiSC, Enneagram, or any other assessment tool) in making employment decisions. Regardless of a person's self-proclaimed type (whose validity is dependent on their own level of objectivity and self-awareness), the ultimate predictor of a person's success is his/her previous behavior in similar situations experienced in the past and his/her interests and aspirations to actually do the work. And since all of us have the ability to tap into each and every one of the various motivations and personality traits, based on whatever situation we have been dealt, it is ineffective to use personality tests/assessments as arbiters of selection decisions. Furthermore, it has been my experience that there are many successful people whose personality types may not align with the archetype associated with their roles. Assessment instruments, when deployed appropriately and focused on growth and development, can be very useful. They are particularly effective at creating awareness, understanding, and empathy. They do this by inspiring dialogue around interpersonal differences, communication style preferences, conflict resolution options, and variances in motivations. The results of these conversations, of course, help to create a more effective and productive work environment where innovation and productivity can thrive.

The above being said, I have included a set of behaviorally- and Enneagram-based interview questions in Appendix D. These are not meant to identify a candidate's type (and are not phrased in such a way), but rather to determine a candidate's emotional intelligence in terms of ability to adapt to different personalities and difficult situations they are likely to encounter in any organization.

NOTE ON DIVERSITY & INCLUSION

Most organizations currently struggle with how to create cultures where diversity is celebrated and all perspectives and insights are welcomed and heard. The findings presented in this chapter can help leaders understand the wide range of different perspectives and gifts that exist in the population (and prospective candidate pool), employees' diverse needs, and how to engage them so that the benefits of diversity are realized.

Chapter 4

Strategic Planning

So far, we have seen how the Enneagram can help managers identify different ways to relate to their employees and ensure that their staff members are effectively motivated and engaged. Individualistic approaches have been recommended for each Enneatype. However, there are also more general approaches that also benefit the team. Strategic planning is a severely underutilized tactic in helping leaders and managers motivate their teams, drive engagement, nurture cohesion, guide decision-making, and resolve conflicts. Too many times, employees are set loose in a role and are expected to "hit the ground running." How many times have we heard (or perhaps even uttered) that in an interview? It's the easy way out, adopting a laissez-faire attitude to management. True leadership, though, involves inspiring people to action, showing them how the roles they perform fit into the achievement of the organization's goals, mission, and vision, coaching and developing them, and removing obstacles so that they can make their magic happen. Furthermore, customizing the experience by allowing as much input as appropriately possible is a key factor in making employees feel included, heard, valued, and committed to the outcome. Let's look at how the Enneagram can help managers and leaders achieve the greatest results in this arena, while optimizing the time they spend in this exercise.

Traditional strategic planning processes involve the senior leadership team of an organization participating in a facilitated retreat over the course of several days (sometimes even stretched out over several months) to discuss their ideas and visions for where they see the organization going and how to get there.

Vision- or goal-based strategic planning approaches include:
- establishing a shared vision and writing an inspiring vision statement
- identifying and crafting a compelling purpose/mission statement
- identifying goals needed to be attained, supporting the mission, while striving for the vision
- identifying approaches/strategies to achieve each goal
- identifying action plans for each strategy
- creating and publicizing a strategic planning document
- monitoring progress and updating the strategic plan, as necessary

Throughout this detailed process, there are many opportunities for personal agendas, interests, and politics to derail focus on the full picture and what is ultimately important. The Enneagram can help guide senior leaders through these landmines and ensure that the best possible outcome is attained and all perspectives are included.

The How and Why: Taking Care of Business With The Enneagram

Let's take a quick look at the nine points of the Enneagram through the lens of strategic planning:
1. Mission, Purpose - What
2. Linkages & Who/How/Why it helps
3. Goals – How/When
4. Unique Differentiator (Quality? Price? Speed?)
5. Research and Due Diligence
6. Contingency Planning
7. Big Picture Planning
8. Span of Control, Governance, Action, Implementation, and Accountability
9. Continuous Environmental Scanning and Calibration

The logical process of strategic planning doesn't follow Steps 1 through 9 of the Enneagram in order, but we can definitely see a pattern emerge when we take a closer look:

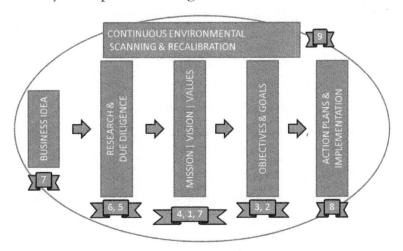

Figure 4-1 | Enneagram-Driven Strategic Planning Model

Step 1: Business Idea

Every business evolves out of a bright, novel idea of how to create a new, different, better, faster, or cheaper product or service that will somehow make the world a better place, at least for someone, if not everyone. This seems like a very natural space to use the strengths of the Enneatype 7:

- Innovation, novelty
- Big picture
- Identifying and taking advantage of new, exciting opportunities
- Ideas
- Optimism
- Future-planning focus
- Brainstorming

Step 2: Research & Due Diligence

Once the idea is envisioned, work must be done to see how viable it is to operationalize and what, if any, competition or other factors exist in the market and environment that may hinder the vision's successful attainment. This lies in the sweet spot of the strengths of Enneatypes 6 and 5 and flows well if we proceed counter-clockwise around the Enneagram symbol:

- SWOT (Strengths | Weaknesses | Opportunities | Threats) analysis
- Contingency planning
- Worst-case scenario planning
- Realism
- Environmental analysis

The How and Why: Taking Care of Business With The Enneagram

- External stakeholders
- Internal stakeholders
- Contingency planning

Step 3: Mission/Vision/Values

Now that we know what the competitive landscape looks like and we've conducted our due diligence, it's time to revisit our initial vision and see if it is still realistic. Then tie in the mission of our specific company and call out how we will contribute to its fruition, along with the determination of our values, norms, and rules of engagement to help guide our actions. As we continue our counter-clockwise journey around the outside circle of the diagram, we stop and engage the strengths of Enneatype 4, then travel up its comfort/security arrow to Enneatype 1, and then traverse its comfort/security arrow to Enneatype 7:

- Mission – what we are here to do; our niche; how we add value; our differentiator; what sets us apart from others; how we are special / different from our competitors (Enneatype 4)
- Vision – the future state as we see it (Enneatype 7)
- Values – core beliefs, operating principles (Enneatype 1)

PRACTITIONER NOTE

A very efficient way of facilitating a team to focus on the development of its Mission Statement is to introduce the following formula to the team members and lead them in a brainstorming discussion of the appropriate words to fill in the blanks:

> *"The (name of the team) team exists to deliver (describe products/services) by (describe major activities performed to create products/services). We do this so that (describe purpose of meeting customers' needs)."*

While the final product may not end up looking anything like this initial statement, it's a very effective shortcut to help get the conversation started and honed.

Step 4: Establishing Objectives and Goals

Resuming our counter-clockwise course, right next to Enneatype 4 on the Enneagram are our next two sequential stops for our strategic business plan. Now that we have clarified our mission, vision, and values, it's time to create concrete objectives and goals that will operationalize how we will attain our mission and vision. This time we need to engage the strengths of Enneatypes 3 and 2:

- Goal-orientation
- Metric-orientation
- Action-orientation
- Linkages/relationships to make it happen
- Identification of needs

This is a critically important step, as these goals will be cascaded throughout the organization. Each department will then operationally define what these objectives mean to the team and how it can contribute to the company's overall goal achievement. Involving teams in the goal-setting process will show team members how their jobs matter to the organization and drive their further engagement and commitment. This, too, is where the age-old SMART technique comes into play, assuring that goals will be as clear and meaningful as possible:

- Specific
- Measurable
- Aggressive, yet Attainable
- Realistic/Results-oriented
- Time-bound

Since most managers and employees experience difficulty in this arena, here is a formula to help facilitate effective goal-setting. Simply select a choice from each column and the goals virtually write themselves!

ACTION VERB	WHAT WILL CHANGE?	SUCCESS MEASURE	DUE DATE
- Achieve	- Loss	- By #%	- By _____
- Attain	- Morale	- By $#	- Each Week
- Decrease	- Productivity	- By # of Points	- Each Month
- Improve	- Profitability		- Each Quarter
- Increase	- Quality		- Each Year
- Lessen	- Sales		
- Lower	- Satisfaction		
- Maintain	- Savings		
- Maximize			
- Raise			
- Reduce			
- Sustain			

Figure 4-2 | SMART Goal Formula

Step 5: Action Plans and Implementation

From our current pit stop at point 2 on the Enneagram (and since we've already recently visited Enneatype 1 in Step 3), it is

time to follow Enneatype 2's stress arrow to Enneatype 8 and engage its strengths in action planning and implementation:
- Focus on the present
- Work through challenges/obstacles
- Execute! Hold others accountable and move them to action
- Action-orientation

Step 6: Continuous Environmental Scanning and Recalibration

Right next door, clockwise, to our last stop on the Enneagram circle is point 9. Once we've implemented all of our action plans, we need to step back and assess how we're doing in the context of our overall environment. This is a natural strength of Enneatype 9:
- Seeing all perspectives
- Balancing, harmony-setting
- Taking in all that is happening around them

This proposed model does not, by any means, suggest that we have to hire or engage people whose strengths are identified in each step of the process. Remember that each of us has access to every one of the Enneagram points and its respective strengths and blind spots. We simply have to remember to engage every one of our "Enneasenses" at the appropriate time to ensure that we are seeing the whole picture and gaining the full perspective of every situation. Once

The How and Why: Taking Care of Business With The Enneagram

a robust strategic plan is in place, it must be disseminated across the organization and referenced often (i.e., via internal communications vehicles and town hall meetings) to remind everyone in the organization why they are there and what they are expected to accomplish. In addition, this model can serve as a grand mediator and arbiter of conflict (does this action/decision support our mission, vision, and values?).

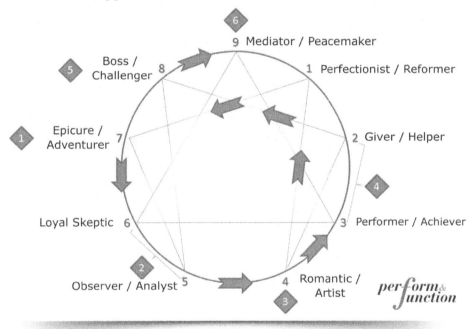

Figure 4-3 | Enneagram-Driven Strategic Planning Flow

PROCEED WITH CAUTION

As companies experiment with eliminating performance review ratings, which may demotivate rather than drive employee engagement and performance, it is important to consider that certain Enneatypes may actually look forward to their annual evaluations and ratings. Specifically, Enneatypes 1, 3, and 5 (the competency triad) may be more drawn to performance reviews where their competence, results, and knowledge are officially and systematically recognized, in comparison to their peers. Leaders and managers can stave off any possible frustration and discouragement caused to their Enneatype 1, 3, and 5 employees by checking in with them to determine how best they can feel that their performance has been truly acknowledged and differentiated from their peers.

Chapter 5

Values

Speaking of values, let's see how the Enneagram can provide organizations with guidance in identifying the right components on which to focus in defining and propagating their corporate cultures.

A major actionable component of strategic planning, that is cascaded and integrated into myriad organizational structures and programs, is the values segment. Organizations spend countless hours of executive brainpower and debate to decide what their values are, or what they should be, to effect a culture transformation and ensure their future existence and success. Values are important because, when implemented properly, they become embedded in the organization's culture (i.e., executive and organizational communications and actions, extrinsic awards), compensation and rewards systems (through the performance management and evaluation processes), employee and leadership development programs (i.e., 360-degree feedback assessments, training classes), and in as many other areas as possible in order to promulgate the norms of the organization. Some organizations do this well, while most do not. What all organizations do, however, is pretty much decide on the same sets of criteria that they deem to be integral to their company's future success. And these ubiquitous criteria happen to align perfectly with the Enneagram. Take a look at the organizational values, norms, competencies, and/or behaviors of current top performing companies and, invariably, a combination of the following will emerge:

Does the Right Thing (Enneatype 1)
- Quality
- Process Improvement
- Modeling the Values
- Ethics
- Compliance
- Mission-Driven Decision-Making

Collaborates With & Serves Others (Enneatypes 2 and 9)
- Empathy
- Customer Service
- Teamwork
- Brings People & Ideas Together
- Builds Relationships and Connections
- Collaboration
- Cultural Competence
- Communicates Inclusively
- Customer-Driven Decision-Making

Drives for Achievement / Results (Enneatype 3)
- Adaptability

The How and Why: Taking Care of Business With The Enneagram

- Flexibility
- Resilience
- Goal-Orientation
- Efficiency
- Goal-Driven Decision-Making

Leads With Courage / Thinks Strategically (Enneatypes 4, 7, and 8)
- Big Picture Vision
- Possibilities
- Creativity & Innovation
- Optimism
- Communicates Directly and Transparently
- Acts Transparently
- Supports and Develops Team

Makes Strategic Business Decisions, Learns & Shares Life-Long (Enneatype 5)
- Observes
- Listens
- Continuous Learning
- Shares
- Asks Clarifying Questions
- Collects Data / Information

Makes Data-Driven Decision | Makes Timely, Well-Informed, and Appropriate Business Decisions (Enneatype 6)
- Risk-Taking

- Decision-Making
- Contingency Planning
- Questions / Challenges then Commits
- Safety
- Accountability

Organization Development practitioners and executives are tasked with facilitating or coming up with their organization's/department's/division's values and norms. The Enneagram can be tapped into as a resource to focus attention on the tried-and-proven factors that organizations keep recreating, renaming, and rebranding. Use the organization's own language and operational definitions to make the values and norms relevant to the team's purpose and meaningful to its people and their roles. This will not only serve as a more efficient exercise, but it will also help ensure that we are being as inclusive as possible and leveraging all the different variables and strengths brought forth through the Enneagram framework.

After identifying which values are most appropriate, relevant, and important for the organization or team, the next step is to personalize or customize these values and interpret them into language that makes sense to the business, industry, and/or team. This can be a great exercise to undergo as a team, so that there is agreement from all stakeholders from the very beginning and everyone is more likely to be committed to the outcome. Engage the team to come up with operational definitions for each of the values identified. Then create norms out of them (or rules of engagement) and make explicit what the consequences for non-compliance are going to be. Then implement and reinforce them! That means calling people out when they are not behaving according to the agreed-upon values and norms. Reward those that do behave in accordance with them. These values can and should be cascaded into the organization's culture by including them in the performance review process. Rate people on how well they are exemplifying the competencies and behaviors associated with these values. Reward them for serving as role models and exemplars. Once they have attained high performance status in their roles (and if they are comfortable doing so), have them serve as mentors to new hires and others who need more exposure to the organization's or team's culture. And don't be afraid to use these values in other aspects of the business, including decision-making, problem-solving, and influencing others.

For example, if "Teamwork" is selected as an important value in the organization, engage the team in brainstorming what this term means and how they will know if they're all performing in that manner. Is it intra-team collaboration? Does it include partnering with external members and stakeholders? To what end? Be as explicit, yet inspirational, as possible and ensure everyone's buy-in to the final statement.

A Fun and Practical Way to Make them Stick

Once team norms are in place, a fun, practical, and non-threatening way to make sure that they "stick" is to assign and use symbols for each norm. I have had great success using stuffed animals as exemplars to represent various norms across all organizational levels, functions, and disciplines. Although I was initially skeptical about introducing toys into conservative corporate cultures, after establishing the facilitator's credibility with the group/team, these tools can easily and naturally be introduced as self-managing norm-keepers. To do this, purchase several medium-sized stuffed animals, each one corresponding to a different norm established and agreed to by the team. For example:

- **Rabbit or Rat** – indicates that the group is going off topic, or getting too far down into the weeds (down a rabbit or rat hole) and away from its goal. This can serve as a great reminder for Enneatype 1s and 4s to avoid getting too detailed or pushing for something to be 100% when 80% will suffice. The rabbit or rat can help remind the team to stay on task and focus on achieving its goal, reinforcing a "focusing on results" norm.
- **Elephant** – represents "the elephant in the room" and grants permission, without repercussions, for a team member to speak the truth that no one else has had the courage or opportunity to bring up to the rest of the team. Enneatype 5s (who tend to see things objectively), 1s, and 8s seem to display an affinity to using this symbolic stuffed animal to bring something forward to the group. The elephant can help to support an organizational norm around integrity and truth-telling.

The How and Why: Taking Care of Business With The Enneagram

- **Sponge or "Sponge Bob"** – reminds people that they need to listen and take in what their coworkers are saying, like a sponge (reinforcing norms around respect, dignity, listening, and not interrupting). This is especially useful when Enneatype 7s may get sidetracked.
- **Monkey** – represents accountability – either taking on the appropriate responsibility for something that rests within our domain or passing the monkey to the person where that responsibility appropriately resides. This may come in handy when Enneatype 2s, 3s, and 9s manifest their tendency to not decline requests made of them, regardless of whether the task rests in their domain; the monkey can then be passed onto the actual responsible party.
- **Devil** – allows someone to take on the necessary role of challenger/questioner/"Devil's Advocate" to ensure that all options are being considered, discussed, debated, and evaluated fully. Enneatype 6s and 8s tend to gravitate towards this role. The devil can represent an organizational norm around innovation and problem-solving.
- **Elmo** – to help keep things moving. It is common for teams with lots of Enneatype 7 energy (or teams who are high in the Thinking center of Enneatypes 5, 6, and 7) to default to their strengths in brainstorming, visioning, thinking, and planning, and run out of time or energy to get to action. A norm that could be adopted by these teams is the calling of "ELMO" – or "Enough,

Let's Move On!" when too much time is being spent in this area. Any team member is empowered and accountable to call "ELMO" whenever the team falls into this unproductive behavior, so that the team can then move into action.

Note that any Enneatype can violate any meeting or organizational norm at any time and that the Enneatypes called out here do not maintain a monopoly on the behaviors and animals with which they have been associated above.

These tools all serve a dual role. They are an up-front visual reminder to the team of their agreed-upon rules of engagement as well as a non-threatening way of reinforcing the team and organizational norms. If someone breaks a norm, the facilitator or another team member can throw the stuffed animal representing that norm at the offender. I have been happily surprised to see team members ask permission to "go down a rabbit hole" for a limited amount of time, at which juncture they seek out the rabbit and hold it while they engage in the detail necessary for the topic of discussion. Once finished, they relinquish the stuffed animal, thus acknowledging and honoring the team norms. I have also been equally pleasantly surprised to see team members eagerly take on the role of enforcing the norms amongst themselves, rather than relying on the facilitator to do so.

The How and Why: Taking Care of Business With The Enneagram

PRACTITIONER NOTE

Competing priorities and ever-escalating demands for higher productivity with fewer resources are inducing angst in many organizations. This may be exacerbated in organizations that tend to nurture cultures where their employees find it difficult to say no to new requests. An interesting solution to help organizations and employees prioritize where and how to spend their limited resources (time, money, headcount) can be found in the use of the tried-and-true Covey (né Eisenhower) Urgent/Important Matrix. Ask leaders to identify the core values of the organization. This could be from formal, published vision and mission statements, operating principles, decision rubrics, goals, etc. Assuming that there is alignment between this philosophy and actual practice, use these as the criteria for what is important to the organization. These can then be superimposed onto the Urgent/Important matrix, whilst respecting some key concepts:

- Important activities pass the test of aligning to values or goals that are critical to the organization's (or person in the role's) success.
- Urgent activities have a deadline associated to them, and may or may not be associated with the person's or organization's strategic remit.

These distinctions can help us group and prioritize activities and asks into the following buckets, which in turn helps us to focus on the most impactful work first:

	URGENT	**LESS URGENT**
IMPORTANT	**1. Do It!** In service of the vision/ mission/values/goals/ operating principles	**2. Schedule It!** In service of the vision/ mission/values/goals/ operating principles
LESS IMPORTANT	**3. Delegate/ Push Back!** What can I delegate to someone else, maybe even to our broader network (internally or externally)?	**4. Don't Do It!** What can I stop doing because it doesn't make sense or add value (any more)?

Figure 5-1 | The Urgent/Important Matrix

Chapter 6

Culture

The simplest way to think about culture is "the way we do things around here." Culture is huge. Culture trumps everything else. Culture mismatches have been blamed for the failures of many attempted mergers and acquisitions – and, conversely, culture alignment is considered a significant factor in successful mergers and acquisitions. Culture is entrenched and intractable. It takes a lot of concerted effort over many years to change culture successfully and pervasively.

Executive coaches are often asked to help out in situations that involve some kind of culture mismatch between the coachee and the environment in which s/he is attempting to operate. Sometimes it's a mismatch that has been tolerated for a long period of time and something has instigated a need to have it addressed at this point. This trigger could be a new manager, a new emphasis on performance management, a budget crisis necessitating higher scrutiny in headcount, a reorganization, a major faux-pas, or visibility to a broader/higher-level audience to whom the non-conforming behaviors are unacceptable at best and insulting at worst. Marshall Goldsmith's *What Got You Here Won't Get You There* is an excellent resource for understanding how behaviors that were once effective and tolerated at one level may no longer work at a higher level.

The Enneagram presents a robust and easily accessible way to address the concept of culture mismatch or clash to individuals who may experience this phenomenon happening to them. There are a few ways it can be innocuously introduced – in team settings or in individual coaching.

Team Settings

A practical way to introduce the concept of culture, so that its repercussions and implications are understood by individuals, is as an extension to team-building (see Chapter 11). This will be more effective when all team members have already established their individual Enneagram type affiliation and have at least some rudimentary understanding of it. This will enable them to compare and contrast their default values and perspectives to those of the organization as a whole and pre-emptively identify and prepare for any clashes. At the end of the session where the group has been introduced to the Enneagram and has completed the "What motivates people?" exercise (or in a follow-up session at a later time to reinforce the learning), lead the team members in a discussion by asking them:

- "Now that you know your individual types and have an understanding of the other eight types, it's time for your final exam: What Enneagram type is this department? What makes you think so? What are the implications to our ability to be effective within this organization?"

- "What Enneagram type is this division/function/group? What makes you think so? What are the implications to our ability to be effective within this organization?"
- "What Enneagram type is the overall company/organization? What makes you think so? What are the implications to our ability to be effective within this organization?"
- "What is the focus and what are the values associated with these types? How do your focus and values integrate with them? Where do you see a potential for mismatch or conflict? How will you resolve this?"

When facilitating this discussion, keep the focus positive, constructive, and productive, to avoid the possibility of degrading to a "below the line" victim mentality. It is imperative to prevent demotivating people who may have the epiphany that they may not be a good match to the culture by having them find ways (via their Enneagram type's wings, arrows, and tri-types) to better align with it.

Individual Coaching

Whereas the team development approach may be more of a pre-emptive effort to help individuals better plan and acculturate to an organization, the individual coaching approach may be more reactive. At this point, the manager, HR Business Partner, executive coach, or Organization Development practitioner has been engaged because of evidence that there is a mismatch between the employee's actions and the way things are expected to be done at the organization. The manager is usually at his/her wit's end by this point, because s/he has already broached the subject with the employee on myriad occasions to no avail. There may also be managers who don't know how to best approach the issue and may seek out additional help to do so.

The Enneagram here, too, can serve as an invaluable resource and shortcut to frame this difficult conversation. A simple and effective way I've found is to ask the individual to identify and write down his/her values. These can be generated by asking:
- "What are your values?"
- "What is important to you?"
- "How do these values show up and play out at work?"

Then, up the ante, by asking:
- "What are your manager's values?

Raise the stakes even further by asking:
- "What are the organization's values?"
- "What does the organization really expect and reward?"
- "How do these values reflect what the CEO expects and how s/he behaves?"

The answers to these last three questions may be different if a disconnect exists between the stated values of the organization (the ones on the posters, brochures, plaques, websites, and recruiting materials) and the way things really are done.

Edgar Schein talks about identifying culture through artifacts, beliefs, and underlying assumptions. Since actions speak louder than words (which in this case means they reflect the true culture), it's important to see how employees are actually behaving. Artifacts are visible clues in the organization that provide evidence of the culture in action:

- What are the norms around meetings? Do they start and end on time? Are they productive and generate action and accountability?
- What do people put on their desks? What do they put on the walls in their offices? What does that reflect?
- How do people communicate with each other? How do they interact outside of work?
- Who are the "insiders?" Who are the "outsiders?" Why? How did they attain that status?
- What is rewarded? What role does tenure play? What about performance?

Ask the coachee about what artifacts s/he sees around the organization that can elaborate on the definition of the company's real culture. Make the connection here between the artifacts, corresponding beliefs, and underlying assumptions represented by them.

Now apply the Enneagram. Relate the coachee's values to his/her Enneagram type affiliation. Ask him/her to identify the Enneagram type of the department and broader organization. Then ask him/her if and how s/he can bridge those gaps. By calling out the similarities and differences between the coachee's values and the organization's values, the coachee can decide for him/herself how feasible it is to alter his/her perspective, behaviors, and expectations appropriately. This usually involves a conversation about patience and "picking your battles." If s/he decides that the gap is too large and that s/he is not ready or willing to do so, the result may be that s/he makes a move to exit the organization and find an environment and culture which is more suitable and aligned. And that's OK.

PRACTITIONER NOTE

For-profit and non-profit organizations are very different. Because of their divergent missions and cultures, they tend to attract different types of employees. For example, I have noted a marked absence and lack of Enneagram Type 4s in the large, for-profit organizations in which I have worked; they seem to be more attracted to creative, mission-driven non-profit organizations . Recall the "What motivates people?" exercise in Chapter 2 and tap into that insight. Which were the last Enneagram type motivations to be identified? Which were the first? See if there's a connection of the early-identified values to the company's culture. Are the values that were last identified (or not identified at all) by the group the ones espoused by the coaching client? How can the coachee tie that initial experience into what is going on for him/her now?

The Enneagram can help individuals to identify the expectations and factors necessary to succeed in their organization and possibly find a pathway to align or temper their own values, behaviors, and expectations to match them. Organizational culture (or at least what the organization wants to signal to the outside world through its marketing department) can be conveyed in its mission or slogan. In

The How and Why: Taking Care of Business With The Enneagram

addition, an Enneagram culture type can be associated with different countries based on their ideologies and practices. The following table presents some examples for consideration and conversation:

ENNEAGRAM TYPE	ORGANIZATIONAL VALUES/ARTIFACTS	COMPANY EXAMPLE	GEOGRAPHY EXAMPLE
1. Perfectionist	Integrity, Ethics, Doing the Right Thing	LEXUS: "The (relentless) pursuit of perfection"	England Switzerland
2. Helper/Giver	Helping Others, Connections, Relationships	AMERICAN RED CROSS: "... exists to provide compassionate care to those in need"	Italy Greece
3. Performer/Achiever	Getting Results, Looking Good, Status	BMW: "The ultimate driving machine" JAGUAR: "Born to perform" "Art of performance"	USA China
4. Artist/Romantic	Being Different/Unique, Authenticity	FIAT: "Driven by Passion"	France Korea Portugal
5. Observer/Analyst	Knowledge, Research, Analysis	CIA: "Our business is knowing the world's business"	Finland
6. Loyal Skeptic	Planning, Risk-Aversion, Safety & Security	VOLVO: "For Life" 3 Core Values: Safety, Quality, Care for the Environment	Germany
7. Enthusiast/Epicure	Fun, Options, Opportunities	PONTIAC: "We build excitement" LAND ROVER: "Go beyond"	Brazil Nevada, USA: "Don't Fence Me In"
8. Boss/Protector	Power, Authority, Control	ALFA ROMEO: "Power for Your Control"	Russia
9. Mediator/Peacekeeper	Aversion to Change, Maintaining Status Quo, Peace & Harmony	SATURN: "Like Always. Like Never Before"	Canada

Figure 6-1 | Enneagram Applied to Culture, Companies, and Countries

Note that Richard Rohr and Andreas Ebert (2001) present their own take on which countries represent which Enneagram type:

Enneatype 1: Switzerland
Enneatype 2: Italy
Enneatype 3: United States
Enneatype 4: France
Enneatype 5: Great Britain
Enneatype 6: Germany
Enneatype 7: Brazil, Ireland
Enneatype 8: Spain
Enneatype 9: Mexico, Austria

Culture Stages

In addition to its application in understanding company/organizational culture, the Enneagram can also be used to improve understanding of differences between the cultures of different countries. Aperian Global's "SCOPE" Model identifies the stages of culture as:

- Seeing Differences (involving cultural self-awareness and inviting the unexpected)
- Closing the Gap (invoking frame-shifting and achieving results through relationships)
- Opening the System (through the expansion of ownership and development of future leaders)
- Preserving Balance (attained through core values and flexibility, allowing adaptation and value-add)
- Establishing Solutions (depending on the development of collaborative solutions through influence across boundaries)

The How and Why: Taking Care of Business With The Enneagram

Note the natural affiliation between these stages and the Enneagram system:
- Enneatype 1's power of discernment comes into play in "Seeing the Differences."
- The "Results through Relationships" component of "Closing the Gap" evokes the strengths of Enneagram Heart Enneatypes 2, 3, and 4.
- "Opening the System," expanding ownership, and developing future leaders lies in the land of Enneatype 5 and its Enneatype 7 and 8 arrows.
- Enneatype 9's natural proclivity to "Preserve Balance" is next.
- "Establishing Solutions" plays to the wheelhouse of Enneatypes 6, 7, and 8.

Although intended and marketed for cross-country cultural comparisons and understanding, this framework can easily be applied to improve cross-organizational (and even intra-organizationally among different divisions, departments, or functions) awareness and work effectiveness. We can all tap into our ability to access each of the Enneagram perspectives within us to successfully progress through the stages of this process and help to guide our clients to do the same.

Chapter 7

Decision-Making, Problem-Solving, and Innovation

When Human Resources and Organization Development practitioners dig deeply into their clients' presenting problems, they commonly discover that trust is the core issue. Eroding trust and fear lead to employee reluctance to contribute, experiment, take risks, and speak up, all of which negatively impact organizational problem-solving and innovation. Not only does this result in employee disengagement and dissatisfaction, but it also prevents organizations from fully tapping into and benefitting from their employees' brilliance and expertise, potentially missing out on many opportunities for competitive advantage.

Fortunately, the Enneagram provides us with a natural, inclusive framework through which we can help organizations, leaders, and their employees to get to feel empowered to make decisions, solve problems, and innovate at all levels. Ideally, when we use the Enneagram for team-building (see Chapter 11), we will jumpstart inter-team member understanding, empathy, and trust-building. Furthermore, we can continue leveraging the Enneagram to provide guidelines and guardrails to employees so that they can feel psychologically safe when empowered to take responsible and acceptable risks in decision-making, problem-solving, and innovating.

To those ends, we can utilize the Enneagram to evaluate decisions or potential solutions to problems and help ensure that we are making the best decision every time. By stepping sequentially and purposefully through the process, we can be sure that we are taking into account all necessary components and factors so that our decision is sound. Now that we understand that we may be heavily influenced by a fixation of our preferred and default Enneagram type, we can unleash the power of the Enneagram to help us combat this inherent bias while leveraging the power and perspectives of all nine types. When faced with a decision of having to choose between competing options (or even evaluating the viability of one option), we can use the robustness of the Enneagram to ensure we are considering all important variables in the equation. We can ask ourselves:

Through the Lens of Enneatype 1:
- Is this the right thing to do?
- Does it support our mission, vision, and values?
- Is it the best quality?
- Does it NOT smell "fishy"?
- Would I be OK (not embarrassed) if it was reported in the media?
- Would I be comfortable explaining it to my children, family, and friends?
- Looking back at the end of my career, am I proud of this decision?

Through the lens of Enneatype 2:
- Is it in the best interest of our stakeholders?
- Does it help solve a problem and/or add value?
- Will it strengthen our relationships with our customers, employees, investors, Board of Directors, etc.?

Through the lens of Enneatype 3:
- Is it timely and efficient?
- Can we afford it? Does it fit within our budget?
- Can it be implemented within our time parameters?
- Will it contribute to the attainment of our goals?
- Will it enhance our image and reputation?

Through the lens of Enneatype 4:
- Is it elegant and unique?
- Does it align with our niche?
- Will our competitors have difficulty replicating it without our resources, Intellectual Property, and talent?

Through the lens of Enneatype 5:
- Is it the logical choice?
- Is there data and research to support its efficacy? Is there data to refute its efficacy?
- Are there other satisfied customers/users/testimonials?

Through the lens of Enneatype 6:
- Is it safe?
- Are there effective safeguards/firewalls/security

measures in place to protect our organization's and our customers' assets, data, etc.?

Through the lens of Enneatype 7:
- Does it allow for future expansion?
- Can we add/build onto it as we grow?
- Does it allow for a flexible environment to take advantage of potential future opportunities and needs?

Through the lens of Enneatype 8:
- Can we control it?
- How much authority and autonomy do we have in its use and administration?
- How much input and influence do we have with the vendor for future updates/upgrades?

Through the lens of Enneatype 9:
- Is it sustainable?
- How harmoniously does it fit with our other systems, tools, and processes?
- How likely are our people/customers to embrace it?
- Is it "green"/environmentally-friendly?
- Will it create a harmonious environment?

Each of these questions can be modified to fit the appropriate decision factors and specific situation. For example, when evaluating a hiring or promotion decision between candidates, alter the questions so that they take into consideration the factors that make sense to that specific instance.

Taking this a further step, we can integrate this framework into a modified Kepner-Tregoe (KT) decision-making model. The KT approach focuses on establishing clear objectives or criteria for the choice, and understanding the level of influence or weight each objective has on the overall decision. It uses a combination of this influence weight multiplied by a performance score for each alternative to indicate 'best performance' against the stated objectives. To counteract the potential for subjectivity (given the fact that bias-susceptible humans select the factors against which the options will be evaluated), dropping in the set of Enneagram-based factors just presented allows us to create a more objective and robust system. This can be used in many different settings to evaluate myriad options, products, services, and vendors. To further minimize the potential for and effects of subjectivity, it would make sense to engage a team of subject matter experts with diverse perspectives to review the choices and come up with consensus (or averaged) weightings and ratings.

For this step, we can use the following scale when determining the Criterion Value Score for each of the Enneagram-based factors:

- 0 = Not applicable / Not necessary
- 1 = Nice to have
- 2 = Should have
- 3 = Must have

The How and Why: Taking Care of Business With The Enneagram

When evaluating the extent to which an option/product/service/vendor meets each Enneagram-based factor, we can use this scale to assign an Option Evaluation Score:
- 0 = Does not meet criteria at all
- 1 = Meets some criteria; Does not meet other criteria
- 2 = Meets most criteria (but not all)
- 3 = Meets all criteria well

The next step is to simply multiply our Criterion Value Score by our Option Evaluation Score. Then add all the products together to come up with the Option's Total Alignment Score. Repeat this for the other options being considered and compare each option's scores, selecting the highest-scoring option.

A sample of what the decision-making template might look like follows. Of course, we may add any additional requirements that may need to be considered, but the Enneagram-based factors provide an excellent and robust starting point. We can use this system to guide our clients to drive the most objective and inclusive decision possible for any given situation.

Criterion	CRITERION SCORE	OPTION 1		OPTION 2		OPTION 3	
		RATING	SCORE	RATING	SCORE	RATING	SCORE
Supports our mission/vision/values			0		0		0
Best Quality?			0		0		0
Does NOT smell fishy?			0		0		0
Comfort with media publicity			0		0		0
Explainable to children/family/coworkers			0		0		0
Future retrospective pride in this action			0		0		0
Solves a problem/adds value			0		0		0
Strengthens stakeholder relationships			0		0		0
Affordable/fits within budget			0		0		0
Implementable on time			0		0		0
Supports our goal-attainment			0		0		0
Enhances our image/reputation			0		0		0
Aligns with our niche			0		0		0
Difficult to replicate by our competitors			0		0		0
Supported by Data and Research			0		0		0
Other satisfied customers/users			0		0		0
Effective safeguards/firewalls/security			0		0		0
Expandable			0		0		0
Flexible environment			0		0		0
Administrative authority/control			0		0		0
Influence over future options			0		0		0
Harmonious fit within our system			0		0		0
Embraceability			0		0		0
Green/environmental			0		0		0
Creates a harmonious environment			0		0		0
OPTION TOTAL			0		0		0

Figure 7-1 | Enneagram-Infused Kepner-Tregoe Decision-Making Matrix

A PRACTICAL APPLICATION

A Research & Development leadership team identified the need to encourage greater innovation within the company's very risk-averse culture. The concept was so foreign to the staff scientists that they asked for guidelines to be used in helping to determine acceptable risk. The leadership team then decided to use the Enneagram to help them operationally define, clarify, organize, and communicate a checklist of considerations to their staff scientists, guiding their innovation agenda. The staff scientists were instructed to ask themselves the following cadre of Enneagram-type based questions to get a full picture of whether their potential new ideas were worth the risk.

APPROPRIATE RISK-TAKING | DECISION-MAKING CHECKLIST CONSIDERATIONS

1. Does this align with our values, ethics, and operating principles?
2. (How) will it impact other areas? What are the potential repercussions on others? How will it affect our stakeholders, network, community, customers, colleagues?
3. Does it support our goals? Is it the most efficient option? How will it affect cost/budget? What is the Return on Investment (ROI) or Return on Value (ROV)?
4. Is this a niche solution? Does it present an opportunity to pursue patent protection? What unique value does this solution bring?
5. Is there data/research/evidence to support that this is the logical action to take?
6. What is my back-up/contingency plan if this fails? What are the consequences if this desired outcome isn't achieved or if we don't take any action?
7. Does this allow growth for/in the future? What are my

other options? What are the likely positive outcomes? What other/new opportunities does this create?
8. Is this within my scope of authority/purview/domain to execute?
9. (How) does this fit within and affect the overall ecosystem?

I have since worked with clients who have simplified this rubric, sometimes selecting three from the list (aligning with their most important organizational values) or encouraging their teams to proceed if their ideas meet any number of them. It depends.

Chapter 8

Influence

Once we have reached the situationally-appropriate decision, we will need to persuade or influence others in the organization to also support and buy into it. Once again, the Enneagram can serve as a valuable asset in this endeavor.

The Hay Group produces a self-assessment instrument called the *Influence Strategies Exercise* that helps individuals identify which of nine influence strategies they tend to adopt (and to consider using others in order to increase their effectiveness). Check them out below, along with their Enneagram correlates:

- Empowerment (democratic involvement in decision-making, recognizing others) = Enneatype 9
- Interpersonal Awareness (identifying and allaying others' concerns) = Enneatype 2
- Bargaining (negotiating a mutually-satisfying outcome, favor exchanging, resource sharing, concessions) = Enneatype 6
- Relationship-Building (rapport-generation, wide network of contacts, socialization, friendliness) = Enneatypes 2, 3, and 7

- Organizational Awareness (identifying and enlisting support of key stakeholders) = Enneatype 3
- Common Vision (showing how personal ideas support the organization's overall goals and direction, appealing to values and principles) = Enneatype 1
- Impact Management (selecting the most dramatic, interesting, memorable way to grab others' attention and present your ideas) = Enneatype 4
- Logical Persuasion (use of logical reasoning, expertise, facts, and/or data) = Enneatype 5
- Coercion (threats, reprimands, pressure) = Enneatype 8

The nine different strategies identified in this model coincidentally relate pretty tightly with an Enneagram counterpart, as reflected above:
- One could argue that the definition of *Empowerment* as "democratic involvement in decision-making and recognizing others" invokes many of the gifts and strengths of Enneatype 9s, the Mediators or Peacekeepers, who, in their comfort arrow, take on the strengths of Enneatype 3s, the Performers, who take on challenging goals and get them done.
- By defining *Interpersonal Awareness* as "identifying and allaying others' concerns," one is reminded of the intuitive gift of Enneatype 2. 2s are aware of others' needs and concerns, even when the others themselves may not have that insight, and take action, whether invited or unwelcomed, to resolve them.

- *Bargaining* is defined here as "negotiating a mutually-satisfying outcome, favor exchanging, resource sharing, concessions." This skillset taps nicely into the strengths of Enneatype 6s, who are acutely aware of the worst-case scenario and develop multiple back-up and contingency plans to address its possibility of occurrence. This natural tendency is invaluable in a negotiation since Enneatype 6s are likely to have planned for every contingency and have a response already prepared.
- *Relationship-building* comes easy for the über-social and charismatic Enneatype 7s, 2s, and 3s. They seem to be described to a tee by this model which calls out the importance of "rapport-generation, a wide network of contacts, socialization, and friendliness."
- *Organizational Awareness* taps into the gifts of tact and diplomacy of the ever-alert and action-oriented Enneatype 3s in "identifying and enlisting the support of key stakeholders."
- The values and principles-focused Enneatype 1s can exercise their strengths in the areas of "showing how personal ideas support the organization's overall goals and direction, appealing to values and principles" in the *Common Vision* tactic of influence. Note that this is also a strength of Enneatype 7s, the comfort/security arrow of the Enneatype 1.
- Enneatype 4s are naturals at utilizing the *Impact Management* technique, which involves "selecting the most dramatic, interesting, memorable way to grab

others' attention and present your ideas," no?
- Who would be better at *Logical Persuasion*, the "use of logical reasoning, expertise, facts, and/or data," than Enneatype 5?
- *Coercion*, invoking the techniques of "threats, reprimands, and pressure," are often associated with Enneatype 8. Although admittedly not the most flattering or positive of attributes, keep in mind that this technique is most effective in crisis situations when action needs to be taken immediately in the face of dire consequences.

When attempting to influence someone, it is best to know the perspective or style to which they tend to default. While attempting to influence *Star Trek*'s Dr. Spock or *Big Bang Theory*'s Dr. Sheldon Cooper with Impact Management may be entertaining to watch, it would not likely be as effective as the Logical Persuasion technique in yielding the desired result (unless the desired result is to annoy them!). Knowing our audience, a cardinal rule in public speaking, also applies to influencing them. When working with colleagues we know well, we know what to include and what to exclude in presenting information to them with which they need to make a decision and/or support our recommendation. This has probably evolved from a history with those individuals and our own unconscious strategy derived from multiple trial-and-error experiences and observations. When we are unsure of how best to approach a new potential ally, it may be helpful to ask others who know or have worked with him/

her to which strategy s/he has responded best. If we don't have the luxury of the acquaintance of any such colleagues, a recommendation that is inclusive of all nine strategies may be successful, since the target to be influenced will respond to at least one of them. I would recommend this approach in new sales calls. Note that identifying what the potential client's needs and pain points are will usually point to which perspective will be most applicable. This strategy also works well when presenting to large audiences, whose constituents will inevitably represent all nine perspectives.

Show how the recommendation or solution:
1. Is the right thing to do. How does its selection and implementation fit with the overall vision, mission, and values of the organization?
2. Addresses their pain points, needs, and concerns. How does it also help to connect to others? How does it meet their needs?
3. Meets the goals of the organization and is in alignment with its image. How will it make the organization, stakeholders, and this decision-maker look good?
4. Is unique, special, and one-of-a-kind, customized for this specific client/need. How is it differentiated from the rest?
5. Is the logical choice. Provide the best, most persuasive, objective data including competitors' and conflicting data.
6. Is the safest choice. How is this solution going to

prevent/thwart potential future threats to the security, safety, and comfort of the organization?
7. Is fun! And expandable! And limitless! How does this option allow for future possibilities and changes?
8. Is controllable.
9. Allows for collaboration and is systemic/inclusive and sustainable.

Imagine how powerful the application of this tool is in the influence realm. Sales is an area of particular potential application. Once a salesperson understands to which of the nine Enneagram types a potential customer relates, s/he can tailor the sales pitch and message to those needs and concerns so that the client has the information deemed relevant to make an informed decision. This should, by no means, be misconstrued as manipulation. It is merely presenting specific data to potential customers so they can make an informed decision with data that is relevant to them. The client still has the ultimate say as to whether or not to go ahead with the purchase. It is simply a more focused and guided approach. And if a salesperson is unsure with which Enneatype s/he is dealing, s/he can create a pitch that addresses the concerns and perspectives of all nine Enneatypes. This is certain to touch on the needs of the client while presenting a comprehensive description of all facets and features of the product or service. This approach can be especially effective if pitching or presenting to a wide audience of several hundred people (i.e., at a conference),

The How and Why: Taking Care of Business With The Enneagram

where all Enneatypes will likely be present.

In sum, let's revisit the decision-making and problem-solving techniques discussed in Chapter 7 and apply them to our sales/influence message here:

1. It is the right thing to do that supports their mission, vision, and values.
- Is it the right thing to do at this time?
- Does it support their mission, vision, and values?
- Is it the best quality for them?
- Does it NOT smell "fishy"?
- Would they be OK (not embarrassed) if it was reported in the media?
- Would they be comfortable explaining it to their children, family, and friends?
- Looking back at the end of their career, would they be proud of this decision?

2. It takes into account and addresses the needs/pain points of their stakeholders.
- How is it in the best interest of their stakeholders (including their customers)?
- How does it help solve a problem and/or add value? For them? For their customers?
- How will it strengthen their relationships with their customers, employees, investors, Board of Directors, etc.?

- How does it address their stakeholders' needs?

3. It takes into account and addresses their organizational needs.
- How is it timely and efficient for them?
- (How) can they afford it? (How) does it fit within their budget?
- How will it be implemented within their time parameters?
- How will it contribute to the attainment of their organizational goals?
- How will it enhance their brand, image, and reputation?

4. It is a unique solution to their challenge(s).
- How is it elegant and unique?
- How does it align with their niche/capabilities?
- How will their competitors have difficulty replicating it without their resources, Intellectual Property, and talent?
- What kind of dramatic presentation can be made to make this memorable, meaningful, and impactful to them?

5. It makes logical sense to do this.
- How is it the logical choice?
- What is the data and research that supports its efficacy?
- Who are the other satisfied customers/users/testimonials?

6. Implementing this solution is a safe bet that keeps us safe.

- What makes it safe?
- What effective safeguards/firewalls/security measures are in place to protect their organization's and customers' assets, data, etc.?
- How does it mitigate their risk exposure?

7. This solution addresses current and future needs.
- How does it allow for future expansion?
- How can they add/build onto it as they grow?
- How does it allow for a flexible environment to take advantage of potential future opportunities and needs?

8. It allows them to own and control their own destiny.
- How can they control it?
- How much authority and autonomy will they have in its use and administration?
- How much input and influence will they have for future updates/upgrades/changes?

9. It is a sustainable solution that supports their ecosystem's balance.
- How is it sustainable?
- How harmoniously does it fit with their other systems, tools, technologies, and processes?
- How likely are their people/customers to embrace it?
- How is it "green"/environmentally-friendly?
- How will it create a harmonious environment?

Integrating these Enneagram-based elements into our proposals, presentations, sales pitches, and communications maximizes our likelihood of success in persuading and influencing others. Regardless of our job titles, roles, or functional alignment, we are all sales people to one extent or another; we only add value and contribute when we "sell" our concepts, ideas, and messages to others.

Chapter 9

Communication, Communication, Communication

While real estate is all about location, location, location, the number one item that is consistently reported as the area in greatest need of focus for organizations is communication. Time and time again, employee satisfaction and engagement surveys reveal that this is an unmet need in companies. Regardless of how proficient executives and leaders are in communicating, there is always an employee desire for more.

As long as we remain unable to read other peoples' minds, the emphasis on communication is critical so that people understand each other better, take action based on the best and most up-to-date information, and minimize unproductive conflict and misunderstandings. Many tools and frameworks have been developed to account for individual differences in communication needs. The variables within this realm include depth of information (big picture versus detail), mode of communication (verbal versus electronic), and context (relationship versus business). The simplest framework I have come across to categorize communication preferences and optimize effectiveness is contained with the DiSC instrument, which aligns well with the Enneagram. In addition, one can use the insights of the Enneagram to help make the DiSC even more meaningful.

DiSC and its offshoots (including BEST, Emergenetics, Insights, and the Four Seasons) categorize human communication needs along certain dimensions:

- Assertiveness in shaping versus responding to environment, including pace of speed
- Acceptance and people-focused versus questioning and logic-focused

Using these variables, we can easily see how the Enneagram types fit within this simple framework, and how the framework's recommendations for optimizing communication can apply to each Enneagram type.

DISC | INSIGHTS CATEGORY	RELATION TO ENVIRONMENT, PACE	FOCUS	MANTRA/ SLOGAN	ENNEAGRAM TYPE
D - Dominance (Fiery Red)	Shapes, Fast	Logic, Questioning	Be Brief, Be Bright, Be Gone!	1,3,7,8
i - Influence (Sunshine Yellow)	Shapes, Fast	People, Accepting	Involve Me!	2,3,4,7,8,9
S - Steadiness (Earth Green)	Adapts, Moderate	People, Accepting	Show me you care.	2,4,5,6,9
C - Conscientiousness (Cool Blue)	Adapts, Moderate	Logic, Questioning	Give me the details.	1,5,6

Figure 9-1 | DiSC and Enneagram Correlates

The Dominance DiSC category, with its need to direct and dominate others, is blatantly applicable to the assertive Enneagram types: the archetypical Enneatype 8 and can also Enneatypes 3 and 7. We may also find some 1s in this territory. Expect a bold, loud, forceful, strong, clear, confident, and fast-paced style of communication, with lots of direct eye contact, body language that leans in towards us, and perhaps even some pointing – especially from the 1s! To best engage with Ds, we need to match their fast-paced, direct, and on point communication style. It is also important to demonstrate our competence and credibility and not provide any unnecessary details (unless probed to do so).

The Influencing DiSC category, whose goal is to interact with others using its optimism and people orientation, is most inclusive of the optimistic Enneagram types found in the Positive Outlook Triad: Enneatypes 2, 7, and 9. Enneatypes 3 and 8 can also be found here, especially if they score highly in DiSC style D as well. Enneatype 4s coupled with a bimodal score of high S may also inhabit this quadrant. Expect animated, friendly, rambling stories and explanations in a somewhat loud and casual/familiar style. Their communication is described as motivational and inspiring. The DiSC-recommended communication strategy for these types is informal, relaxed, and sociable. There will likely be lots of smiling and expressive gesturing. Brainstorming is likely to occur with these predominantly Extraverted types. However, in order to capitalize on the ideas of brainstorming, it will be necessary to follow up and create a concrete plan of action with deadlines, especially when dealing with Enneatypes 2 and 7.

The Steadiness DiSC category aptly describes the withdrawn Enneagram types: Enneatypes 4, 5, and 9. Additionally, we will see Enneatype 2s (who we would also expect to score highly in DiSC style I) and 6s (who would score highly in DiSC style C, too), here. Expect soft, low voice tones that are warm, methodical, and full of details, and small hand gestures. The recommendation here is for relaxed and patient communication to match their style. When communicating with these types, creating a secure and stable environment is key. It may be difficult to read these types if they are non-expressive and "poker faced." These types also need to be sincerely appreciated, with a demonstration of their importance to the organization. If there are changes, they need to be approached carefully with enough lead time for these types to prepare for them.

The Conscientiousness DiSC category supports Enneatypes 1, 5, and 6; two-thirds of the Competency Triad (Enneatypes 1 and 5 plus Enneatype 6) or two-thirds of the Dutiful Triad (Enneatypes 1 and 6 plus Enneatype 5). Expect a quiet, deliberate communication style in a monotone, precise, cool, and aloof tone. Body language will be controlled, with direct eye contact, and minimal hand gestures. Think Lilith from *Fraser*, Sheldon from *Big Bang Theory*, or Spock or Data from *Star Trek*. Here, communication needs to be factual, supported by evidence, and to the point. The strategy here is to be prepared with data and evidence to back up our premise, expect and not fear their criticism, and be as precise and focused as possible.

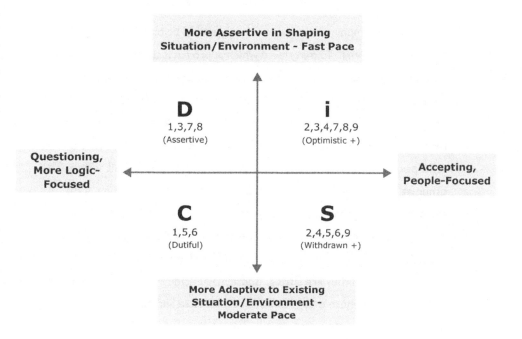

Figure 9-2 | Enneagram Types Plotted on DiSC Axes

PRACTITIONER NOTE

Most people exhibit combinations of these dimensions in their styles; we are style blends, usually of the DiSC styles adjacent to (not diagonal from) each other. Check out Appendix C to see how some of the DiSC style combinations can play out in each Enneatype. For example, Enneatype 1s can be seen to score highly in Conscientiousness and Dominance. Enneatype 2s will score highly in both Influence and Steadiness. Enneatype

3s, 7s, and 8s are likely to score highly in both Dominance and Influence. Enneatype 6s can score high in Influence, Steadiness, and Conscientiousness. We are likely to see high scores in Steadiness and Conscientiousness in Enneatype 9s.

As such, communication strategies may need to be blended or tailored to the individual as well. To determine which approach is the most appropriate for an individual, it can be helpful to simply ask the subject to which DiSC style s/he most relates. This will help determine which communication strategy to engage when working with him/her. When working with a team or group, assign each person by his/her Enneagram type to a DiSC style pod/table. For example, have Enneatypes 1, 7, and 8 sit with each other at the "D" table; Enneatypes 2 and 3 at the "i" table; Enneatypes 4 and 9 at the "S" table; and Enneatypes 5 and 6 at the "C" table. Proceed through an exercise of identifying the characteristics of each DiSC style and ask the class participants whether they affiliate with the DiSC type of the table at which they are sitting. Some may decide to move to one of the adjacent tables, where they feel more comfortable and experience a better fit/alignment. Take this a step further and have each DiSC pod flipchart:

- their group self-perception of their own DiSC type
- their group's perceptions of the other three DiSC types
- potential challenges other DiSC styles may experience when working and communicating with them
- how they prefer others address these challenges with them
- a slogan, tag-line, and logo that represents their DiSC style

Report out this exercise by asking a volunteer representative of each DiSC pod to present the flipchart to the rest of the class. During the report out, have the presenter skip his/her pod's perceptions of the other DiSC styles until the other respective DiSC pods present their self-perceptions.

The How and Why: Taking Care of Business With The Enneagram

Check in with each of the other three pods for their perceptions of the presenting pod's characteristics. Make sure to appreciate each pod's contributions and insights at the end of its presentation through class applause.

Combining the simplicity of the DiSC system with insights from the Enneagram yields much deeper conversation and understanding about similarities and differences in communication styles and needs than just DiSC alone. For example, when leading a discussion about high Dominance/Directive styles, a facilitator can tap into and validate the knowledge that Enneatype 8s tend to communicate via debate, in order to get to truth. Furthermore, they expect others to debate them back. If others don't engage with them in the debate, they run the risk of the Ds/8s thinking of them as weak and writing them off. The facilitator can also mention and validate that Ds/8s don't intend to come across as intimidating. In fact, it actually upsets them when they find out that this perception of them may exist and that they may have hurt significant others in that way. Use this as an entryway to gauge the D's/8's comfort level at inviting/allowing others to let them know when this might be happening. Check, too, to see if 1:1 Enneatype 1s and 6s, Social 2s and 7s, and Self-Preservation 9s may relate well to this style. These subtypes tend to resemble Enneatype 8 and its needs.

Facilitators can draw connections to the i's high likelihood of Extraversion (as is the case with Enneatypes 2, 3, and 7). This insight reveals a proclivity for these Influencing types to enjoy engaging in brainstorming activities. The danger lies in potential lack of execution after the brainstorming. Also, more Introverted types may not understand that the Extraverts are just brainstorming and may misinterpret this activity as a fully-fledged thought or decision that needs to be acted upon. Facilitators can call out the importance of confirming whether brainstorming or action planning is happening, and establishing and tracking progress towards the achievement of action items and next steps. Check, too, to see if 1:1 Enneatype 4s, Social 5s, 6s, 8s, and 9s, and Self-Preservation 4s and 6s may respond well to this style. These subtypes tend to resemble Enneatypes 2, 3, or 7 and their respective needs.

Insight into Enneatypes 4 and 9 can provide additional flavor to discussions around the S's need for stability and aversion to change. Facilitators can lead discussions here around the S's/4's/9's valuation of diversity and the positive attributes of each option. This may contribute to a difficulty in making decisions, especially if those decisions result in a change or threat to their status quo and equilibrium. Communication strategies need to address this need, as the same topic may need to be raised on different occasions over a period of time so that comfort can be harvested and the change accepted. Bringing up a change just once isn't enough for Cs; repetition and allowing time for integration are vital. Check, too, to see if 1:1 Enneatype 2s and 7s and Self-Preservation 2s and 6s may respond well to this style. These subtypes tend to resemble Enneatypes 4 or 9 and their associated needs.

Enneatypes 1, 5, and 6 like details, aligning them with DiSC type C. Insight into why they like details can help people interacting with them, by guiding them to which details they will likely be drawn. Enneatype 1s focus on the details pertaining to the ethics, values, morals, and doing the right thing appropriate to the situation. Enneatype 5s want to know they have all the intelligence available about the issue, good and bad. Enneatype 6s gravitate towards details that will help them feel comfortable, safe, and ready to survive the worst-possible case scenario. Note that the countertypes of Enneatypes 1, 5, 6 are their 1:1 Subtype, so they may not align as closely to

The How and Why: Taking Care of Business With The Enneagram

the DiSC style C needs. Check, too, to see if Self-Preservation Enneatype 2s, 3s, 4s, 7s, and 8s, Social Enneatype 4s and 6s, and 1:1 Enneatype 7s may relate and respond well to this style. These subtypes tend to resemble Enneatypes 1, 5 or 6 and their corresponding needs.

We can also turn to the Enneagram to help us in becoming more effective in our interpersonal communication styles. For example, Enneatype 1s may be likely to unconsciously appear judgmental or even condescending in their language or undertones. They may tend to use words such as "should" and "ought to" and may even point in an accusatory manner. Some of these behaviors can be off-putting to others. Realizing they have these tendencies can help Enneatype 1s control and manage them, increasing their effectiveness. Given the higher occurrence of Myers-Briggs ISTJs in Enneatype 1s (and 6s), they can tap into their strength in "thinking and processing before they speak" and focus on details to ask themselves if what they're about to say could be (mis)construed as judgmental. Is there a different way to present their opinion? Should it be spoken at all? They will also benefit from understanding their preference for closure and that they may ask many probing questions designed to satisfy their need to determine whether this is the right (or safe, in the case of 6s) thing to do. When communicating with Enneatype 1s in writing – their preferred mode, allowing for processing – avoid typographical, grammatical, and formatting errors. These may cause the Enneatype 1s to focus on those distractions rather than the content of the communication. Provide as many details as possible and present a logical argument with no extraneous information.

Enneatype 2s, in their attempts to please and be liked by others, can sometimes come off as ingratiating, overly complimentary, manipulative, inauthentic, and Pollyannaish. They may also tend to sugarcoat negative or tough issues and avoid confrontation in an attempt to nurture connections and relationships. To that end, they are also known to subjugate their needs in deference to the needs and desires of others. Self-awareness that they have these tendencies can help Enneatype 2s counteract them and be taken more seriously by others. When communicating with 2s, others should remember to authentically acknowledge their help, support, and contributions. There will likely be a lot of emphasis on connection and the nurturing of the relationship. Depending on the nature of the relationship, one can also ask the Enneatype 2 what s/he needs and remind him/her take care of those personal needs as well. Given the higher occurrence of Myers-Briggs ENFJs in Enneatypes 2 and 3, we can use this knowledge to recommend that they make sure that their verbalized thought processes are taken as the brainstorming they are, instead of well-formulated plans of action. They can prevent misunderstandings by others by explicitly stating when a thought becomes an actual course of action in which others need to participate. When dealing with more logical types, it will become necessary for Enneatypes 2 and 3 to suppress their value-orientation in favor of more rational approaches to decision-making.

Enneatype 3s, in striving for efficiency, may cut to the chase and think/talk too fast for others. They may use language alluding to competition and winning/losing. They also tend to take on too many things and not ask for help from others. Advice for Enneatype 3s would include slowing down and allowing others to help them. When communicating with Enneatype 3s, care must be taken to respect and not tarnish the image they are projecting/protecting. It's also a good idea to acknowledge their contributions and successes, in an authentic way. Of utmost importance, don't waste their time – arrive on time, be efficient in managing time in interactions with them, and leave on time. The guidelines described above in the Enneatype 2/ENFJ discussion will apply to Enneatype 3s as well.

The How and Why: Taking Care of Business With The Enneagram

Enneatype 4s will tend to use dramatic, sometimes melancholy language involving feelings and emotions. Listen for comparisons to others and to glorified/romanticized, lost, past situations. Care must be taken to pay attention to Enneatype 4s and to authentically make them feel unique and special. Given the higher incidence of Myers-Briggs INFP with Enneatype 4s, expect that they will need their alone time to process and recharge, and, as such, may be more responsive to written communications (such as email or even handwritten notes). Give them time to come up with their creative solutions before asking/expecting them to share with others. Appreciate them for their unique contributions. INFP is the polar opposite of the western world standard expectation (ESTJ), so it makes sense that Enneatype 4s don't feel like they fit in. Call out and nurture these differences since diversity is so important to counteract groupthink and encourage innovation. Enneatype 4s will have to flex the most in getting their point of view across to the other types. Still, it's a good practice for them to focus on what is present rather than for yearning for what is absent or lost in the past.

Don't expect Enneatype 5s to say much, unless it's an area in which they are experts and an environment in which they feel comfortable and safe to do so. Especially in more known, intimate groups. Then, expect a fount of knowledge to overflow. Enneatype 5s will typically seem reserved and keep information to themselves. When it is shared, it may sometimes come across as being pedantic or condescending (and that may or may not be the intent!). Given a higher presence of INTJ at Enneapoint 5, written communication in advance of when a response is needed is highly recommended. Appropriate thought, processing, and preparation can then take place. Provide a logical and real deadline, as that is motivating. When communicating with Enneatype 5s, keep it short, logical, and to the point.

Enneatype 5s are great at the paradox of deciphering data (details) and making sense of its patterns (leveraging their MBTI "N"). So they do look for details. However, social interactions can drain the precious energy levels of Enneatype 5s, so respect those boundaries. In turn, Enneatype 5s will find that people won't have to keep coming back to them for more information if they provide them with what they're looking for, with enough detail – counter to their "N" nature – in the first place.

MBTI-wise, Enneatype 6s seem to congregate in the ISTJ and ISFJ space. Given they are "head" types, I recommend adhering to the ISTJ characterization, similar to Enneatype 1s. The guidelines described above in the Enneatype 1/ISTJ discussion will apply to Enneatype 6s as well. They, thus, also share the proclivity towards DiSC styles S and C. In addition, Enneatype 6s will tend to ask a lot of clarifying questions to get the details they need to feel safe and secure and decide whether others are trustworthy. They will need processing time to decide, so written communication may be more conducive, especially if they want to go back and verify something. Growth and development for Enneatype 6s in the communication arena can come from practicing to trust themselves and others, letting go of their doubts, and becoming aware of and eliminating their own second-guessing nature.

Enneatype 7s may tend to self-reference, coming off as self-centered. This may be compounded by a proclivity to distraction ("Squirrel!"). Like Enneatype 2s, 7s can also appear Pollyannaish. Development here can come in the form of practicing focus (especially on the present, real situation) and inclusivity of others and their perspectives and experiences. It is interesting to note that the MBTI preferences of the adventure-seeking Enneatype 7 (ENTP) are the exact opposite of the safety-oriented Enneatype 6 (ISFJ). When communicating with them, focus on the big picture and

The How and Why: Taking Care of Business With The Enneagram

opportunities, rather than on details and limitations. It is also important to have patience and perseverance.

Enneatype 8s tend to favor militaristic language and communicate through debate to get to the truth. Many are also fond of using very colorful language (ok, cursing!). True to their ENTJ Myers-Briggs style, they tend to prefer one-on-one, in-person interactions that are short, logical, and to-the-point. They can come across as loud, passionate, and even bully-like. As such, Enneatype 8s need to take care to assess their impact on others – how they are being perceived and received by others in that instance – and change their approach to be more effective in that specific situation. When interacting with Enneatype 8s, others need to stand up to them and match their big, strong energy, or risk being perceived as weak and written off by them.

A practical approach to communicating with Enneatype 9s is to raise the issue or question and revisit it several times with/to them. This helps to counteract the Enneatype 9 avoidance of conflict (the notion that "If I ignore the initial request, it will go away and I won't have to say no or deal with it"). In addition, recall that Enneatype 9s tend to affiliate with the ISFP Myers-Briggs phenotype. The Introversion preference can connote high mental activity, some of which is never ultimately externalized. Introverts sometimes think about the response they will provide and practice it in their minds. This is such a significant process that they may feel that they have actually externally delivered the decision/communication, when, in reality, they have not yet done so. Revisiting the issue with them will help to externalize and verbalize their internal thoughts. Enneatype 9s will tend to exhibit warm, friendly, go-with-the-flow, non-confrontational communication, focused on the other party (this is less true with the self-preservation versions of this type). When communicating with Enneatype

9s, provide them with details that align with their values. Although providing direction to them can help free Enneatype 9s from the tyranny of having to make decisions between seemingly equally-valuable options, care must be taken to not be dictatorial in the process. Growth and development for Enneatype 9 communication effectiveness stems from their working on their comfort and self-confidence in voicing their own opinions.

Note that these generalizations will not apply to every Enneatype and will probably be less true for those Enneatypes whose subtype is a counter-type (see Appendix B). Recall that the Introversion preference on the MBTI tends to correlate to the Self-Preservation subtype, while the Social and Sexual/1:1/Transmitting subtypes tend to correlate to Extraversion on the MBTI.

Providing these guidelines and insights to our clients and mentees can help them become more effective and confident in their communications, presentations, and overall "executive presence."

Chapter 10

Executive Coaching and Development

Debriefing enough 360-degree feedback reports and contracting in enough executive coaching engagements will surely manifest some recurring patterns and themes. The Enneagram can be a very useful tool for executive coaches to use in helping identify and jump start their clients' development activities. In the table that follows, let's take a look at how four Enneagram subject matter experts group the development needs and focus areas of each Enneagram type.

The first step in any type of coaching engagement, or any OD intervention, is some type of assessment of the current state. Most often this is a 360-degree feedback survey report, although sometimes it can be as simple as an observation from the client's manager. Having a multi-rater report allows the subject and coach insight into how different people perceive him/her and whether there is a consensus in themes that may appear in his/her behavior that contribute to or detract from the client's effectiveness in his/her role. Remember the Johari Window discussed earlier in Chapter 2?

	POSSIBLE FOCUS AREAS	IDEAL ENVIRONMENT	HELP THEM SEE
ENNEATYPE 1	• Listening; Understanding • Appreciating; Become more consistently compassionate and attuned to others • Being Right; Continuously improving themselves on a continuous basis • Relaxing; Having more fun; Feeling more serene, especially when mistakes are made or feeling out of control • Setting limits on thier responsibilities; Acknowledging their own mistakes to help them relax	• Positive vision • High standards • Honesty • Fairness • Clear, explicit channels of authority and structure	• There is more than one right way • Mistakes are part of the processs
ENNEATYPE 2	• Focusing inward, not on others • Being fair, balanced, equitable • Feeling less exhausted and depleted; saying no without feeling guilty/anxious/angry • Taking care of themselves first so that they can better help and serve others; Depending less on others' responses and relying more on their own sense of real inner strength • Developing relationships where others can truly be depended upon • Setting limits to prevent over/underestimation of worth	• Personal contact and appreciation • Reassurance of positive outcome of disagreement • Clear job description • Warmth and friendliness	• What they need • Not everyone enjoys as much personal contact as they do
ENNEATYPE 3	• Collaboration vs. Competition • Exploring and re-framing Success vs. Failure • Feeling vs. Doing • Feeling more successful without constant pressure of proving themselves; Relaxing and just "being" without needing to impress others • Having better, more meaningful, and longer-lasting relationships; Experiencing selves at a deeper level • Identifying what they really want for themselves, apart from belief in what social context-based goals should be	• Regular recognition and rewards, clear purposes and goals • Results, action, the bottom line	• Additional input is needed before plowing ahead
ENNEATYPE 4	• Appreciating themselves in the present • Eliminating drama and longing for something else • Learning more about themselves at deepest levels and becoming more truly self-accepting • Being less volatile, emotional, reactive • Making lasting, sustainable connections with others that don't always have to be deep, meaningful interactions • Feeling more capable of making things happen and manifesting dreams rather than feeling like things happen to them • Attending to the task at hand while acknowledging their own feelings • Finding meaning & authenticity in their own work	• Connection and warmth in personal interactions, creativity and insight • Interpersonal interaction	• Criticism of their job performance is not a criticism of themselves • Their special contributions to their jobs
ENNEATYPE 5	• Relating to others publicly while respecting their own needs for privacy • Gathering and sharing information • Truly knowing themselves, using a systematic framework • Better understanding and anticipation of others' feelings; Feeling more comfortable and be more predictable in social interactions • Better organizational acknowledgment for their talents and skills	• Respectful of boundaries • Learning and education opportunities • Opportunities to work solo • Limited surprises	• The importance of their ideas and visions to others

The How and Why: Taking Care of Business With The Enneagram

	POSSIBLE FOCUS AREAS	IDEAL ENVIRONMENT	HELP THEM SEE
ENNEATYPE 6	• Reality Fear Factor • Relating to others without alienating them • Trusting themselves and others • Feeling more secure, certain, and confident; Truly trusting themselves and others to make good decisions and be accountable • Being less reactive and more in control of themselves • Reducing their need to hide reactions by not hiding and compounding anxieties • Eliminating their need for reassurance prior to moving forward; Developing their own authority	• Where rules are not arbitrarily changed • Solid, unpretentious leadership • Open, honest communication about work happenings	• Fears are warranted • Proceeding one step at a time is OK
ENNEATYPE 7	• Reality checks • Getting things done • Learning something exciting and personally beneficial; Transforming ideas into reality • Reading others better and developing deeper and more consistent empathy; Being taken more seriously by others • Feeling more complete as a person • Eliminating the re-framing of problems in a positive light	• Exciting and new opportunities • Support of the development and sharing of their new ideas • Tolerant of the use of their charm in people, contact and communication	• When they are needed to commit
ENNEATYPE 8	• Redefining concepts of leadership and power • Focusing on the content of what is being said, not seeing them as personal attacks; Allying leadership with their organization and empowering others • Listening • Journaling • Knowing the truth from the widest possible perspective; Understanding others psychologically • Feeling less guilty for their own behavior and less responsible for other people • Feeling stronger even when feeling vulnerable/weak; Managing their vast self-energy without imploding/exploding	• Full disclosure (good or bad) • Clear boundaries within which they can work autonomously • Direct, respectful, and fair	• Their forcefulness and need for its moderation
ENNEATYPE 9	• Realizing/acknowledging their own needs • Their ability to see the big picture, priorities at work getting clear agreement • Expressing themselves clearly and directly; Increasing influence and authority; Developing strong, deeply-held sense of personal power to feel empowered to take effective action • Transforming conflict into deeper and more connected relationships, rather than avoiding it • Working with other people from a sense of fully understanding themselves and others	• Support and structure	• Conflict and change as natural and necessary parts of progress

Consolidated and adapted from the works of Ginger Lapid-Bogda, Mary Bast and Clarence Thompson, and Tracy Colina.

Figure 10-1 | Executive Coaching Focus Areas (continued)

360-degree feedback is an ideal way for a participant to gain insight into some blind spot areas and make decisions about which perceptions s/he may want to work on changing. It may also prove beneficial to supplement a 360-degree feedback survey with an Enneagram assessment of the client's type. This could be done to provide an additional data point and further insight into the motivation or reason behind some of the destructive or derailing behaviors that can manifest themselves on these reports. Keep in mind that we are all in different stages of development and integration in our personal growth journeys. In our less healthy/integrated/developed states, we may continue to rely on behaviors that have worked for us in the past and at which we have become experts. These are our strengths. Overutilization of strengths, or using them inappropriately in situations requiring a different approach, leads to failure and derailment. This is how an overused strength can become a weakness ... or an "area for development" if we want to put a more positive spin on it! This is also a great way to show our coaching clients how "dialing back" their strength can lead them to be more effective in certain situations in which they may have previously failed. Remind them, too, that they have an entire repertoire of tools in their toolkit from which they can choose. Different problems require different tools to solve them. If they continue relying on the same action, tool, strategy, or approach, they run the risk of failure and succumbing to the definition of insanity (where we keep doing the same thing while expecting different results).

Let's explore how this may play out:

- Enneatype 1's over-reliance on perfection may make them overly critical, demanding, inflexible, and unrealistic in the workplace. This may show up as difficulty in meeting goals in a timely or fiscally- responsible manner.
- Enneatype 2's need to be liked may lead to an inability to say "No" to others and therefore take on too much work that can't be accomplished. This, in turn, can lead to their burnout and/or their letting others down when the work isn't accomplished.
- Enneatype 3's need to achieve can also lead them to take on too much, which can result in their cutting corners to get things done on schedule. This could lead to harming their reputation, which is of extreme importance to them.
- Enneatype 4's need to be different and unique, along with their penchant for deep feeling, emotion, and meaning, may frustrate their more traditional co-workers who don't see the value in "stopping to smell the roses." They may experience difficulty in connecting with their coworkers and establishing the deep, meaningful relationships that they crave with them.
- Enneatype 5's need for data and analysis can lead to analysis paralysis and no action. They may be perceived as avoiding their coworkers, in favor of data, spreadsheets, and computers, and of hoarding information.

- Enneatype 6's need for comfort and security can lead them to have a reputation as difficult, negative, paranoid, or sometimes even be seen as conspiracy theorists.
- Enneatype 7's need for novelty, excitement, and openness can lead them to not meet deadlines or be seen as flaky and not serious or committed.
- Enneatype 8's need for authority, control, debate, challenge, conflict, and protecting their people can lead them to be seen as bullies.
- Enneatype 9's need for peace, balance, harmony, and stability can make them seem risk- and change-averse. They may also be perceived as indecisive, based on their ability to see positive characteristics in all options, leading to difficulty in choosing just one.

In debriefing 360-degree feedback surveys, verbatim comments from the raters can oftentimes provide intriguing insight into the motivation type of the leader being assessed. This is especially true if multiple raters are commenting on the same behaviors, traits, and competencies, both positively and negatively. There have been many times when this insight has pointed to a participant's probable Enneagram type, which then must be validated with that subject. The Enneagram system provides a way to focus on the real, underlying issue at hand, and not just the surface/resultant behavior. Using the Enneagram as a follow-up to a 360-degree feedback survey enhances the subject's understanding of the reasons behind the others' perceptions of him/her. In addition, it provides immediate development pathways that can be undertaken by a subject who is interested and ready to participate in further development to become even more effective.

PRACTITIONER NOTE

Mario Sikora (2007) has compiled a pretty comprehensive list of potential derailers, by Enneagram Type. A helpful exercise is to provide coaching clients with this type of list and facilitate conversations around which of these have already been brought to their attention, either through their own self-awareness or by trusted others. Then develop a plan of action (such as the "In-the-Moment Practices" presented later in this chapter) to prevent these from negatively impacting their careers and relationships.

Enneatype 1 Potential Derailers:
- Meritocracy – earned status vs. popularity/politics
- Unwillingness to change – others should change
- Seeing the world as black and white – no grey
- Too serious – stiff, detached, not fun
- Perfectionism – focus on mistakes, 100% completion
- Needing to be right – personal solution is the only right way; others are inferior, affront

Enneatype 2 Potential Derailers:
- Breaking boundaries – uninvited intrusions
- Histrionics – inappropriate/overly emotional responses
- Playing favorites – attending to a ranked order of people, issues based on perceived importance
- Worrying about other people's problems instead of own

- Needing to be liked by others, possibly resulting in anxiety, conformity, self-sacrifice, and insincerity
- Tending to take a supporting role by advising, supporting, and/or manipulating (rather than leading from the front)

Enneatype 3 Potential Derailers:
- Spin and wanting to look good at the cost of omitting less flattering details
- Seeming superficial, disingenuous, untrustworthy, and unknowable by trying to be all things to all people
- Self-promoting, attention/recognition-seeking
- "Individual Contributor Syndrome" – pacesetter; Taking on too much
- Speed – lack of attention to detail

Enneatype 4 Potential Derailers:
- Rebellion for rebellion's sake against authority and the status quo
- Making it different/more complicated
- Aggressive overcompensation due to frustration over being misunderstood
- Insistence on being right, leading to defensiveness and hostility against other perspectives
- Lack of confidence and decisiveness
- Dramatic displays of emotions and exaggeration
- Resentment of others' accomplishments and achievements

Enneatype 5 Potential Derailers:
- "Analysis Paralysis"

The How and Why: Taking Care of Business With The Enneagram

- Not nurturing relationships
- Lack of awareness of surroundings and own impact
- Needing to show off intelligence / "know-it-all"
- Hoarding information

Enneatype 6 Potential Derailers:
- Pessimism – focus on problems, complaining, and what could go wrong, rather than solutions
- Suspicion and doubt of good will, intent, and motives of others
- Holding back due to fear of taking risks
- Indecisiveness/distrust of decision-making
- Combativeness / "Devil's Advocate" towards change and outsiders
- "Dog-with-a-bone" Syndrome – relentless persistence in getting point across

Enneatype 7 Potential Derailers:
- Talking too much and not censoring/thinking through ideas
- Failure to follow through
- Hyperactivity, impulsiveness, and distractedness
- Avoidance of negativity and unpleasantries
- Always wanting something else

Enneatype 8 Potential Derailers:
- Bullying
- Volatility/anger and overwhelming/intimidating others
- Needing to be right
- Needing to be "the Boss"
- Rough around the edges

- Impatience and impulsiveness

Enneatype 9 Potential Derailers:
- Holding back due to lack of confidence or fear of being perceived as arrogant
- Conflict avoidance
- Passive aggression – getting their way through inaction
- Fuzzy around agreements and details
- Losing temper after letting unresolved conflicts build
- "Nice Guy Syndrome" - lacking the "killer instinct" sought in leaders

(Adapted from Sikora, 2007)

In cases where traditional 360-degree feedback collection may be too invasive, intrusive, or disruptive to the organization's operations, other options exist. The Hogan Assessment is one such viable alternative, as it takes a subject's self-assessment and extrapolates how these self-reported behaviors can actually be perceived by others. This is based on a large database of correlated self-reported "identity" characteristics versus others' perceptions of the subject's "reputation," showing how they can be strengths in some situations and potential career derailers in others. Coupling this instrument with a validated Enneagram assessment (such as the Integrative Enneagram Questionnaire) is doubly powerful and insightful as the two systems overlap and align quite nicely:

The How and Why: Taking Care of Business With The Enneagram

HOGAN PERSONALITY INVENTORY	HIGH HOGAN SCORE	ENNEAGRAM TYPE	LOW HOGAN SCORE	ENNEAGRAM ARROW
ADJUSTMENT	Handles pressure well, even-tempered, calm handles change well	Integration/maturity level	Moody/temperamental, easily irritated with others, sense of urgency, internalized criticism	Integration/maturity level
AMBITION	Self-confident, leader-like, competitive, energetic	3 8	Lack of energy, status quo, low focus/vision	9 (stress) 5 (stress)
SOCIABILITY	Outgoing, gregarious, approachable, attention-seeking	7, 8 2	Understanding, independent, works well alone, socially reactive	5 (comfort/stress) 4 (comfort)
INTER-PERSONAL SENSITIVITY	Builds coalitions, earns others' trust, thin-skinned, conflict-averse, reliant on others' opinions	2 3, 9 4, 7	Cold, tough, critical, skeptical, forthright, argumentative, task-oriented	8 (stress) 6 (comfort/stress) 1 (comfort/stress)
PRUDENCE	Dependable, reliable, rule-complaint, organized, thorough	1 5	Flexible, non-conforming, open-minded, impulsive, impatient with details	4 (stress) 7 (stress)
INQUISITIVE	Quick-witted, visionary/big picture, strategic, over-analyze	7 6 9	Focused, not easily bored, implementation-focused	1 (stress) 3 (stress) 6 (stress)
LEARNING APPROACH	Formal education, insightful, up-to-date	1, 5	Hands-on/experimental, skills application, practical, narrow interests, unclear goals	7 (comfort/stress)

Figure 10-2 | Hogan Personality Inventory and Enneagram Correlates

Note the first Hogan Personality Inventory factor of "Adjustment." That factor is defined as the degree to which someone appears self-confident, accepting of oneself, and calm/stable under pressure. This factor differs from the others in that it is the best predictor of the likelihood that derailer behaviors may show up (a low score in Adjustment would predict a higher likelihood of derailer behavior occurrence, whereas a middle or high score would foretell the opposite). For this reason, I would equate "Adjustment" on the Hogan to "healthiness" or "level of integration" on the Enneagram, which gives insight into a person's degree of fixation on their primary Enneagram type and ability (or lack thereof) to appropriately access the other Enneagram perspectives.

Also note that when the high scores on the Hogan Personality Inventory are matched to Enneagram types exhibiting those strengths or positive attributes, the low scores on the HPI automatically align to that type's stress or comfort/security point/arrow (although most are stress points).

If a practitioner has the luxury of using both of these assessment instruments to facilitate a subject's development (or even, ideally, an actual 360-degree feedback survey), it will become evident with more and more practice that combining the insights from these instruments can create a more honed and appropriate development plan and coaching focus for an individual than using just one of these instruments alone. The more reports we see and work with, the more connections we will be able to make between the instruments, and the more valuable and meaningful insights we will be able to generate in our clients. Let's see how this plays out with the Hogan Derailers (part of the Hogan Development Survey):

The How and Why: Taking Care of Business With The Enneagram

HOGAN DERAILER	DESCRIPTOR	ENNEAGRAM CORRELATE(S)
BOLD	Self-confidence, entitlement, unwillingness to admit mistakes or listen to advice/feedback	8 , 7 → 1
MISCHIEVOUS	Charming, risk-taking, impulsive, limit-pushing	7 , 5 → 7
COLORFUL	Expressive, overly dramatic, attention-seeking, management by crisis	7 , 3 (also 4)
IMAGINATIVE	Thinking and acting in creative, unusual, odd ways	7 (also 4)
DILIGENT	Meticulous, precise, critical of others' performance	1
DUTIFUL	Ingratiating to boss, eager to please, reluctant to take independent action/ rock the boat	2 , 6 , 6 → 9
EXCITABLE	Moody: Enthusiastic, then disappointed	8 , 2 → 8 , 1 → 4
SKEPTICAL	Cynicism, distrust, doubtful of others' true intentions, feeling mistreated	6 , 9 → 6
CAUTIOUS	Unassertive, risk-averse, fear of criticism/failure/making mistakes	6 , 1 → 4 , 9 → 6
RESERVED	Keep to oneself, indifference to moods/ feelings of others; avoidance of meeting new people	5 , 1 → 4 , 8 → 5
LEISURELY	Independent, ignoring others' requests, resentful of persistence	9 , 1 , 7 → 1 , 9 → 6 , 5 → 7 , 3 → 9

Figure 10-3 | Hogan Derailers and Enneagram Correlates

Hogan methodology classifies the Bold, Mischievous, Colorful, and Imaginative factors as "moving against" components. This aligns directly with Enneagram theory's assertive/aggressive/expansive Hornevian Triad of Enneatypes 3, 7, and 8 (as reflected in the chart above). Hogan's "move with/towards" group of Diligent and Dutiful also aligns perfectly with the Hornevian Compliant/Idealistic/Abiding/Dutiful Triad of Enneatypes 1, 2, and 6 (also shown in the chart above). Less commonality can be found in the Hogan-attributed "moving away" grouping of Excitable, Skeptical, Cautious, Reserved, and Leisurely to the Hornevian

Withdrawn/Detached/Resigned Triad of Enneagram types 4, 5, and 9, unless we incorporate those types' connections to their stress and comfort points.

Once a coaching client's Enneagram type is identified, the coachee's focus generally veers towards growth and development. Providing a coachee with the following amalgamation of Enneatype-related mantras and questions from various Enneagram practitioners can provide a great start in this arena. Ask the coachee to review them and select which ones are most meaningful, applicable, and helpful to his/her particular development needs. This supports the coaching principle that a coachee is more likely to subscribe to a decision or path that s/he comes up with him/herself (rather than having a coach prescribe it). Ask the coachee when these reminders may be most meaningful. At the beginning of the day? At the end of the day? To guide a journaling exercise? Right before interactions and meeting with others? After these? Coaching clients have been especially receptive to this simple and effective focusing/reminding practice.

In-The-Moment Practices:

Type 1:
I am perfect enough. We are all perfect and worthwhile as we are, regardless of perceptions of right or wrong.
- Is this person's perspective just another way of

approaching/perceiving the issue and not necessarily automatically wrong?
- Am I being (too) judgmental in this situation?
- What right do I have to judge this situation?
- How would I feel if someone judged me / spoke to me / treated me / thought of me the way I am doing to this person right now?
- What other information do I need to determine if this other person is also right?
- Does this have to be done 100%? Or is this a situation where 80% is good enough and pursuing 100% would become counter-productive (in time and effort exerted, relationships tried and tested, deadlines not being met)?
- Am I being too rigid/strict in this? How can I permit myself to relax on this?
- In what ways can this other person ALSO be right?
- Why am I really feeling resentment right now? What is really the cause of it? How can I let it go?
- How can I make this fun?
- Am I attentively listening to the others' perspectives and consciously trying to see how they can work/be right?
- Am I appreciating the others' perspectives as a complement to my own?
- Is it really worth "being right" in this situation? What are the potential consequences of my pushing this?
- How am I contributing to this problem? What is my part in this?
- Is this really my monkey? Has anyone invited my

- involvement/input on this?
- What is good/positive about this current situation? What else?

Type 2:

I am receiving and I accept love. We are all loved for who we are, not for how much we give. Giving and receiving is a natural flow. No one is indispensable; that is OK.

- What are my needs in this situation? How can I take care of myself?
- Is my helpfulness being perceived/experienced as intrusive by the recipient?
- Is my giving nature being exploited/taken advantage of?
- Did I say "Thank you" genuinely for the compliment/gift I received without dismissing myself and/or my actions?
- Am I giving and receiving equally?
- Is this really my monkey? Has anyone invited/asked for my involvement/input/assistance on this?
- Am I really qualified and currently able to provide the best help in this case?
- Am I being fair, balanced, and equitable or am I playing favorites?
- How can I say no to this without feeling guilty, anxious, and angry?
- Who can I truly depend on?
- Does it really matter that these people like me?

Type 3:

I believe in myself. I can now be invisible. We are all loved for who we are, not what we can do, achieve, or earn/buy. Everything gets done in its own, natural order and time – we can't force it to get done. Slow down and smell the roses!

- What really matters here?
- How can I create a win-win in this situation?
- Am I burning any bridges by doing this? Am I leaving any dead bodies in my wake?
- How can I be more patient in this situation?
- Am I taking enough time to recharge? How is my work/life balance?
- What am I feeling about this right now?
- What relationships am I harming? How can I nurture them instead?
- Where can I integrate time to slow down and take inventory of my feelings and environment?
- How can I be more collaborative in this situation, instead of competitive?
- What does success really look like?
- Do I really need to prove myself and impress these people?
- What do I really want for myself that is not a socially-mandated outcome?
- What part of my self-image do I feel is being questioned or attacked here? Is this valid?
- What can I control in this situation/environment and how can I focus on making sure it is successful?

- Does it really matter that these people revere me?
- Do I really need to work at this pace/speed? What am I compromising or sacrificing because of this?

Type 4:

I can hear your story. We are all loved, completely whole, and interconnected.

- What's good about this present situation?
- Is this the right time for me to react or can I delay my reaction until my emotions are better controlled?
- Am I focusing on the present and avoiding getting drawn into the past?
- How can I make this ordinary situation more meaningful?
- Is this dramatic reaction really necessary and appropriate?
- How can I eliminate my longing for something else and instead appreciate what I have right now?
- Does this interaction really need to be a deep connection?
- How can I affect this situation and the outcome?
- How can I maintain my uniqueness in this situation, yet still interact and contribute?
- Is this really my monkey? Does this really have anything to do with me?

Type 5:

I know enough. There is a natural and sufficient supply of life-sustaining resources; staying engaged in life will provide access to them.

- Could my current withdrawal in this situation lead to

increased intrusion?
- Do I really need to know this?
- What am I feeling right now? What feelings am I trying to compartmentalize/avoid?
- How can I best participate in this interaction? How does shying away from it hinder my success?
- Is this a demand or a request?
- What are the others around me feeling right now?
- Am I totally present and connected in this moment?
- Is my retraction actually ending up expending more of my energy?
- How can I relate to others publicly while still maintaining my need for privacy?
- How can I best share my knowledge so that others don't impose on my privacy?

Type 6:

I protect my world. It is natural to have faith in ourselves and trust each other.
- How can I use this limited information to move forward courageously?
- Is this a "real" dangerous or fearful situation? What do others think/feel about it?
- Am I staying busy to reduce my awareness/experience of my anxiety?
- What are some other possible positive and realistic alternatives?
- How can I trust myself in this situation?
- Am I alienating others right now with my concerns?

Type 7:

I am grateful for this life. To fully experience life, I have to live in the present and be present.

- Am I being present in the here and now?
- What negative options or emotions (pain, fear, restlessness) am I avoiding/not considering?
- Am I totally focused on the task at hand?
- What obligations am I putting off to which I should be attending?
- Who am I forgetting or letting down?
- What do the others want to do?
- Am I approaching this situation realistically or in an inappropriately fantastic way?
- What should I be focusing on to get done right now?
- How can I transform this idea into reality?

Type 8:

I am magnanimous. We are all inherently innocent and can naturally and objectively sense truth.

- Am I listening to and being open to others' different positions and different energies?
- How am I being perceived and responded to?
- Have I given the others in this meeting an invitation and permission to challenge me and/or let me know if my energy is getting too powerful/overwhelming?
- Are others feeling open and engaged or closed and fearful? Am I actively checking their body language and asking for others' input?
- Am I being guided and controlled by my gut instinct

and drive for action? Am I pausing and breathing deep into my belly before reacting? Have I considered the "Heart" and "Head" consequences, both operational and interpersonal?
- Have I asked for and looked at other more moderate (less extreme) options and possibilities that may be better or more applicable to this situation?
- How is my volume compared to others' in this meeting?
- How much air time am I taking up in this meeting? How can I positively and constructively engage the others in this meeting to contribute and participate?
- How can I redefine my concepts of leadership, power, and authority?
- Is this really my monkey? Has anyone invited my involvement/input on this or am I imposing it?

Type 9:

I am calm and peaceful. We are all unconditionally and equally loved; our worth comes from within.
- What are my own needs in this situation?
- What do I really think about this? What is my position on this issue? What is my agenda?
- What are my boundaries, limits, and priorities?
- Am I expressing myself, my opinion, and my needs clearly and directly?
- How can I engage in and transform this conflict into a more connected relationship?

(Adapted from Andrea Isaacs, 2010)

Another way to leverage the Enneagram with leaders, as a framework for their development, is to approach the coaching from the perspective of business leader competencies needed to succeed in any organization. This can be accomplished by asking the coachee to list all of the critical factors necessary for an organization's success. The Enneagram Institute recommends the following way of interpreting the Enneagram system to this end:

- vision and confidence (Enneatype 8)
- the ability to bring people together and to listen to them (Enneatype 9)
- ethical standards and quality control (Enneatype 1)
- the ability to serve people and anticipate their needs (Enneatype 2)
- promotional and communication skills (Enneatype 3)
- a well-designed product and a sensitivity to its emotional impact on individuals (Enneatype 4)
- technical expertise and innovative ideas (Enneatype 5)
- teamwork and self- regulating feedback (Enneatype 6)
- energy and optimism (Enneatype 7)

Ask the coachee to self-assess himself/herself along these dimensions. Conduct a mini 360-degree feedback survey (or interviews) to determine in which of these areas the coachee could benefit most from further attention and improvement/development.

Note that the activities and practices recommended for each Enneatype's development and growth are directly related and connected to the traits and strengths of the Enneagram type immediately adjacent clockwise to that Enneatype:

- Enneatype 1s have already mastered the Enneatype 9's ability to scan the entire environment and see how all the components fit together. This has been enhanced by the Enneatype 1's strength at differentiation, which the Enneatype 9 needs to learn to develop in order to move to decision and action.
- Enneatype 2s have already mastered the Enneatype 1's ability to discern differences and are able to determine exactly what different people need and how to address those needs to enhance and nurture relationships. This is what Enneatype 1s need to learn so that they can consider the importance of relationships and/or other factors in trumping the need to be right or 100% complete.
- Enneatype 3s are already experts at the Enneatype 2's ability to connect and network. They need to learn how and when to "stop and smell the roses" and pay attention to their feelings and needs, something that Enneatype 4s do quite well.
- Enneatype 4s know how to tap into their Enneatype 3 wing to get things done. They need to learn when to disengage from their intense feelings and emotions and become more objective, something they can pick up from the Enneatype 5's ability to compartmentalize and analyze.
- Enneatype 5s know about emotions (at least academically) and have mastered keeping them in

check. They can grow by tapping into the Enneatype 6's mastery of planning and action for changes and possibilities, based on all of their research and analysis.
- Enneatype 6s are already great at analyzing and researching to plan for and assure their safety, security, and comfort. They can benefit from the Enneatype 7's prowess in positive outlook and seeking out possibilities.
- Enneatype 7s have a proclivity for assessing multiple options and possibilities to determine the most fun and exciting choice and need to tap into the Enneatype 8's power of actual execution on one of them, rather than just coming up with the brilliant idea.
- Enneatype 8s already know how to have the fun (check out their loud, hearty laughter!) for which Enneatype 7s are so notorious. Enneatype 8s can benefit from the Enneatype 9's ability to slow down and seek out peaceful, mutually-agreeable systemic solutions, rather than more forceful alternatives.
- Enneatype 9s already know how to manage (read: suppress) their anger and energy (traits typically associated with Enneatype 8s) and can benefit from Enneatype 1s ability to differentiate between options and take action on one of them.

A PRACTICAL APPLICATION

A coaching engagement with an Enneatype 3 client proved to be very eye-opening for her. She realized that the image she was trying to portray was not who she really was. Furthermore, the energy projecting that image was not producing the desired results she wanted, in terms of her work relationships and success. She even realized that the behaviors she didn't like in others were the very ones she was prone to exhibiting herself! She was then able to reframe what success meant to her and realign her priorities to be more comfortable and accepting of her true self.

A coaching engagement with an Enneatype 1 client resulted in her gaining greater self-awareness. She did this by picking up cues from trusted others pertaining to when she might be having unrealistic expectations about ideal/desired/perfect states that were not operationally feasible. She would then snap out of her "fixation," joke about her "1-ness" coming out, and compromise on a more realistic outcome.

Note that the success of any coaching engagement (or change initiative) is predicated on the readiness, openness, and willingness of the client to be ready to change, to want to change, and do the work necessary to change. In far too many instances, particularly in conflict- and feedback-averse corporate cultures and environments, their career-limiting behaviors are left unattended to and unmentioned. There are no repercussions or incentives (or even, sometimes, awareness of the offending behaviors) to change. That is an unfortunate detriment to all parties involved.

ANOTHER RECOMMENDATION

Earlier in this chapter, we discussed how coaching engagements and leadership development programs typically kick off with some sort of assessment – usually a 360-degree feedback survey. These assessments result in the identification of a few areas for development. Even the highest-scoring High Potentials have some areas for improvement – and this is surfaced through rank ordering the scores from the 360-degree feedback respondents. The effectiveness of the 360-degree feedback survey is dependent on the openness of the survey subject to receiving the feedback, taking it to heart, and his/her willingness and dedication to take action based on it. Many of these well-intentioned efforts fail to achieve their optimum potential for a variety of reasons, usually involving lack of follow-through on next steps by the subject. To buck this trend, I always recommend that the subject engage his/her respondents and key stakeholders in his/her development. Assuming that the feedback generated from a 360-degree survey is going to instantly create self-awareness and counteract decades of its deficiency is a pretty arrogant and lofty expectation, no? The 360-degree feedback survey definitely opens the door to development, but more assistance is needed. The subject can't do it alone! One of the follow-up actions that has been well-received, and proved to be very effective, is an email sent by the subject to his/her respondent list thanking them for their interest and participation in his/her development. The subject provides a summary of the findings, including areas of identified strength and development, verbatim themes, and response rate. Even more importantly, s/he publically notifies the raters about which development areas s/he will be focusing and goes one step further to *invite these key stakeholders to assist in his/her development* by pointing out in-the-moment examples of where s/he can behave more effectively. This action shows the survey respondents that their efforts and input were not in vain and that something is being done with the data. They also have "skin in the game" to help affect and effect the behavioral changes for which they asked. Now the subject has allies in his/her development and those allies have joint visibility and accountability for the subject's success, rather than being uninvolved critics on the sidelines.

To further solidify the learnings and garner deeper support for his/her development, the subject is encouraged to hold "reboot meetings" with his/her key stakeholders. The intent is to restart the work relationship and develop the operating norms and guidelines that may have been missing, or never explicitly addressed in the first place. Samples of the communication, as well as the questions to ask in the reboot meeting, follow:

"Thank you to all who took the time to complete my 360-Degree Feedback Survey. I really appreciate your insightful and constructive comments and am integrating them into my development plan. To this end, I am sharing with you a summary of my results as well as my focus for development. I am also inviting you to help me in my development journey. When you see me exhibiting less than ideal behaviors in the development areas I have identified, please let me know immediately (if we're in a private setting) or shortly thereafter (if we're in public). To this end, I plan on meeting with each of you to ensure that we are on the same page in our interpersonal professional relationship – I look forward to enhancing and optimizing our work relationships!"

Reboot Meeting Questions:

- What are the major goals on which you are currently working?
- What are some of your biggest challenges to achieving these goals?
- In which of these goals do/will we have opportunities to interact? What do/will you expect of me in these interactions in terms of:
    o   Outcomes
    o   Turnaround time
    o   Communication
    o   Milestones
    o   Follow-up
- How do you best like to be communicated with? In person? Email? Telephonically? Instant Messenger?
- How often should we set up 1:1 check-in time to revisit our work and status updates? Daily? Weekly? Biweekly? Monthly? Quarterly?
- When we inadvertently frustrate or are in conflict with each other, how will we let each other know? How will we resolve these frustrations/conflicts?
- What are some of your hot buttons or pet peeves I should avoid?
- What code can we use in public situations to alert each other of a better way to handle the current situation

without embarrassing each other?
- What's important to you? What are your primary values? Why is your work meaningful to you?

The data generated from these questions can be captured in a Stakeholder Analysis document that the subject can populate and reference prior to each future interaction, to remind him/herself about what's important to the key stakeholders and guide his/her interaction with them. It can be as simple as:

STAKEHOLDER NAME	ROLE(Title/ Responsibility)	RELATIONSHIP (Boss/Peer/ Customer/Direct Report)	KEY GOALS, ISSUES & CONCERNS	COMMUNICATION & INFLUENCE STRATEGY

Figure 10-4 | Stakeholder Analysis Matrix

Want to make it more meaningful? Consider prioritizing your stakeholders and corresponding strategy based on how much impact they have on your ability to achieve your objectives. Assess your stakeholders through a lens of organizational power and influence over your project and goals. Those with high influence should be managed closely and kept informed, whereas those with lower influence should still be kept satisfied and monitored with minimal effort.

Note how some of the answers generated in the Reboot Meeting can lead to the subject's deeper understanding of his/her key stakeholders' motivations which may be reflective of their Enneagram types. This will reveal to the subject how to best interact with these key stakeholders in the future. This information can be captured in the "Their Key Goals, Issues, & Concerns" and "Communication & Influence Strategy" columns to be referenced by the subject as reminders prior to future interactions with those stakeholders.

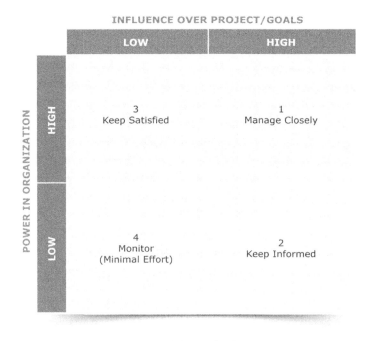

Figure 10-5 | Power/Influence Matrix

A PRACTICAL APPLICATION:
DEEP DIVE INTO THE LEADERSHIP CIRCLE PROFILE

The Enneagram and Leadership Circle Profile: Connections and Complements

People have a variety of resources available to them when they decide to undertake their self-development journeys. Myriad assessments exist to help us become more self-aware, the first step in building up emotional intelligence (EQ). As with any "soft science," it is challenging to measure EQ, its improvement, the extent that emotional intelligence is a success factor for leadership excellence, and if it has an(y) effect on business success.

To this end, the Full Circle Group has conducted its own research in this arena, collecting and analyzing data that indicates that leaders with a specific profile tend to lead their organizations to fiscal success. Specifically, those leaders who score in the top 10% of what they categorize as "creative behaviors" (when compared to a norm group of their peers), and with a minimum of what they classify as "reactive behaviors," tend to lead the organizations in which they work to the top 10% of revenue generation, when compared to their competitors.

Your stuff is your stuff. For life.

Organizations use a variety of tools, models, systems, and frameworks to assess their employees' personalities, strengths, values, motivations, leadership potential, leadership patterns, communication styles, conflict resolution modes, spirit animals, etc. When overdone and not strategically deployed, employees can grow cynical, and even skeptical, especially when their companies only implement these as one-time team-building events rather than long-term investments in mindset shifts or frameworks through which to interpret and facilitate business operations.

Another point of resistance can be encountered when people don't want to take these assessments for fear of being "put in a box" or labeled, or that this will somehow be used against them. This line of thinking doesn't take into consideration that all of us are already in boxes. These boxes contain "our stuff" that we have each collected since our childhoods. Our stuff is comprised of mindsets, tools, tactics, and behaviors we have amassed and developed to survive our childhoods. And since we have had such a long time to live with our stuff, we have built some pretty strong muscles and easy lines of access to these default mechanisms. Understanding what these unconscious, comfortable tendencies are, along with what may trigger these reactions, actually helps people to break out of their self-imposed boxes. What some people don't realize is that others are able to see "our stuff" more easily and more "objectively" – admittedly through their own lenses – than we can. All of the instruments already referenced can help us to see ourselves the way others already perceive us to be. Having this insight frees us to be able to consciously decide which behavior in our repertoire is the most appropriate and effective to use in any given situation – whether that may be our favored default or another.

Those of us fortunate enough to have had the opportunity

to take multiple assessments over time, including receiving 360-degree feedback (from our peers, bosses, direct reports, customers, and others), will tend to notice how the same themes may keep popping up. The severity and frequency will hopefully diminish over time, especially if we continue to work on "our stuff," and it's important to recognize that our stuff is our stuff for life. Our goal is to learn to manage our stuff so it doesn't take over our lives in inappropriate, ineffective, or unfortunate circumstances. It also helps if we know all of the other "stuff" that is available to us. Let's see how the Enneagram-infused Leadership Circle Profile helps us do this.

The Leadership Circle Profile was created incorporating many of the other different personality theories, systems, frameworks and models that preceded it. The Enneagram is one of those systems, and can be easily seen in its mechanics. The goal of the Enneagram is to enlighten us to our unconscious operating system and to find ways of integrating all the lesser developed/accessed elements of our personality in order for us to be more aware and effective human beings. When we have developed and integrated these pathways, and can use them consciously and effectively, we become more effective in our relationships and in life. The Leadership Circle's version of integration is our ability to spend most of our time in the Creative space, while minimizing any unconscious delving into our Reactive tendencies. The Reactive tendencies are not bad, per se, as they have gifts of their own and accomplish certain necessary goals. However, they are not as productive or sustainable long-term, as they tend to drain us of our energy and not reinvigorate us and prevent us from achieving a state of flow, as the Creative behaviors do.

We can relate the Reactive hemisphere of the Leadership Circle to the greatest fears of each Enneagram type. Conversely, we can relate the Creative hemisphere of the Leadership Circle to each Enneatype's virtues:

STYLE	REACTIVE | FIXED (FEAR)	CREATIVE | GROWTH (VIRTUE)
1	Criticism due to own fear of not being good enough	Pursuing and modeling/leading others in the pursuit of excellence (not perfection)
2	Helping others and making oneself indispensable to them for ultimate fear of being unloved by them	Motivating and serving others, without any expectation of reciprocity or acknowledgment
3	Being insignificant and useless	Achieving results, healthy (to self and others)
4	Dramatic reactions and constant comparisons to the past, to counter fear of being without identity	Pursuing own passion(s)
5	Social isolation to prevent being/feeling dependent, exhausted, without resources	Objectivity and proactive information gathering and sharing
6	Being alone in a threatening world	Productive insight and planning
7	Non-committal and positive re-framing to prevent self from being limited or in pain	Inspiring others to pursue visions of innovation and flexibility
8	Bullying others to prevent them from seeing own vulnerability	Making things happen, without anyone feeling intimidated
9	Passivity in response to turmoil or feeling being controlled	True systems thinking, incorporating inclusion and consensus

Figure 10-6 | Enneagram Styles and Related Reactive Fears and Creative Virtues

The Leadership Circle Profile model was built so that we can get insights into which development path to take by "folding the taco" from the Reactive hemisphere into the Creative hemisphere, both across the equator line and diagonally across. This provides a diagonal pathway from the Task hemisphere to the Relationship hemisphere (or vice versa) as well as the option to stay within the same hemisphere if you "fold the taco" across the equator line. What I have noticed in my own debriefs of leaders who have taken the LCP are the following patterns (focusing on reducing the Reactive tendencies through use of the Creative behaviors):

TYPE	REACTIVE	CREATIVE
1	Critical Perfection Arrogance, Autocratic/Ambition	Courageous Authenticity | Integrity Caring Connection | Fostering Team Play | Decisiveness | Achieves Results Community Concern | Sustainable Productivity Selfless Leader | Balance | Composure
2	Pleasing Arrogance	Purposeful & Visionary | Achieves Results | Collaboration | Mentoring & Developing Courageous Authenticity | Community Concern | Personal Learner
3	Ambition Driven	Strategic Focus | Systems Thinking | Balance | Selfless Leader | Composure Mentoring & Developing | Interpersonal Intelligence | Purposeful & Visionary | Sustainable Productivity
4	Distance/Critical	Courageous Authenticity | Integrity
5	Distance Arrogance	Personal Leader | Composure | Community Concern Courageous Authenticity | Community Concern | Personal Learner
6	Belonging Conservative	Systems Thinking | Decisiveness | Strategic Focus | Interpersonal Intelligence | Selfless Leader Achieves Results | Decisiveness | Caring Connection | Fosters Team Play
7	Pleasing Arrogance/Autocratic Ambition/Driven	Purposeful & Visionary | Achieves Results | Collaboration | Mentoring & Developing Personal Learner Systems Thinking | Strategic Focus | Purposeful & Visionary
8	Autocratic Arrogance Critical	Balance | Composure | Sustainable Productivity | Selfless Leader Courageous Authenticity | Community Concern | Personal Learner | Composure Integrity | Courageous Authenticity
9	Passive Pleasing	Sustainable Productivity | Community Concern | Composure | Balance | Selfless Leader Purposeful & Visionary | Strategic Focus | Achieves Results | Collaboration | Mentoring & Developing

Figure 10-7 | Leadership Circle Profile Creative Behaviors and Reactive Tendencies by Enneagram Type

Fortuitously, Marlene de Lange, a South African Organization Development consultant, uses both the Enneagram and Leadership Circle Profile in her executive coaching engagements. Her experiences, research, and analysis have yielded the following insights and findings, as they relate to verbatim comment analysis:

TYPE	HIGHLY CREATIVE LEADERS	HIGHLY REACTIVE LEADERS
1	True to own values and standards Humble Provides guidance and positive, rational feedback Acts with honesty and integrity Enforces slid disciplines, practices, and processes Lifelong learner Respectful Looks for ways to make things more efficient Calm and collected way of leading Needs to create more space for conversation (talk less) Is too humble Micro-manages; Needs to trust the team more Needs to be less operational and more strategic	Strives for excellence - does not accept mediocrity Calm and level-headed Focused Hard-working Slow decision-making Aloof Needs to be more of a team player Needs to focus more on developing people Too negative and critical Needs to think more big picture Needs to trust people and delegate more; stop micro-managing Takes setbacks personally Unaware of own impact Needs to connect more and be more accessible Needs to expand influence beyond technical High distance, critical, arrogant
2	Lives/role models values Humble Elicits great loyalty in teams Builds relationships Passionate and driven Caring and respectful Encourages others to thrive Addresses issues head-on Coaches and mentors team Visionary and knows how to get things done Needs to manage conflict sooner Acts inconsistently Get more well-versed on technical aspects of role Be more bold and courageous in sharing ideas	Mentors people speaks up for the needs of the people Passionate about people Empowers people Narrow focus/silo Waits for consensus Gets too much into the detail Passive- lacks ambition and drive Doesn't project enough strength High pleasing, belonging, passive
3	Leads by example Authentic servant leader Competent and able to integrate complexity Very supportive Optimistic and confident Builds and inspires teams Results-driven without sacrificing people High standards Able to assess, make quick decisions, and take action Dynamic and innovative leader Too hard on self; doesn't celebrate results Takes on too much	Dynamic, creative, and inspiring Strong strategic thinking Drives delivery Cool and rational Deep passion Works in isolation Too guarded - needs to show people who they are Over-commits, takes on too much, and lacks balance Disengaged from the team Indecisive Doesn't share knowledge and ideas Too single-minded/focused Doesn't delegate/prioritize enough High Distance, Arrogance, Driven
5	Performs with integrity Leads by example Gets things done Passionate Down-to-earth and humble Task/results-oriented Needs to delegate/share more Needs more compassion and patience Needs to be more people-focused Works too hard/long hours	Responds to challenges creativity Delivers high quality results High standards Hard worker who never misses deadlines Responds quickly Technical visionary Needs to adopt a more strategic perspective Start trusting the team Too much into the detail Improve ability to inspire and build teams Develop people Panics and stresses too much Is too"black-and-white" Needs to take more personal interest in people High distance,critical,arrogance,controlling

Figure 10-8 | Leadership Circle Profile Verbatim Themes by Enneagram Type (deLange, 2019)

The How and Why: Taking Care of Business With The Enneagram

TYPE	HIGHLY CREATIVE LEADERS	HIGHLY REACTIVE LEADERS
6	Elicits loyalty Prepared to address the elephant in the room Warm and supportive, very engaging Really cares, Empathy Very insightful, Demands evidence and data Insecure, projects onto others May come across apologetic	Checks in with others Creates structure and consistency Uncertain Victim mentality, Over-emotional Comes across as not grounded Micro-manages High passive, distant, critical, controlling
7	Passion, energy, enthusiasm Visionary Positive attitude Support, guide, and empower Collaborative Open, honest, transparent Constructive conflict management Pushing boundaries Listen and consider others' views Talk less	Inspirational Visionary who spots opportunities Challenges the status quo Generating new ideas Consider realistic stepping stones Be more tactful Over-commit and candy coat Distracted Value diverse perspectives Be more prepared to collaborate Too judgmental of others Follow-through, detail High Distant, Critical, Arrogant, Driven
8	Asking difficult questions Passion Open and honest Giving feedback Raising difficult questions Pushing for results Empowering others Firm and decisive Not warm enough - smile more Trying to win every debate Cynicism and sarcasm Disengaged at times	Challenging others to think differently Expressing views Being courageous Energy and drive Too short-term focused Engaging harshly Not listening Over-controlling Unilateral decision-making Forcing own ideas High Passion, Driven, Controlling, Authoritative
9	Supportive, generous Calm and objective Quiet pillar of strength Visionary Decisive Humble Empowering others Leads by example Avoids confrontation Avoids difficult decisions	Knowledgeable Calm Diligent Humble Not compassionate enough Too cautious Monitoring trivial things High Passive, Distant

Figure 10-8 (continued) | Leadership Circle Profile Verbatim Themes by Enneagram Type (de Lange, 2019)

*Note the absence of data for Enneagram type 4, due to the scarcity of this style in for-profit organizations and the sample pool

R. Karl Hebenstreit, Ph. D.

FINDINGS BASED ON LEADERSHIP CIRCLE PROFILE VERBATIMS, BY ENNEAGRAM TYPE

Enneatype 1s tend to score high in Perfection and Critical in the Reactive hemisphere. For 1s, the pathway is straightforward: Directly across from Critical in the Reactive space are Courageous Authenticity and Integrity in the Creative space. This invites Enneatype 1s to diminish Criticality by exploring more productive, positive, and constructive advice while being courageously authentic and maintaining their Integrity (the high sides of Type 1). Another pathway for Enneatype 1s to explore is to traverse diagonally by "folding the taco" across the equator line from Perfection (low side of 1) in the Task hemisphere to Caring Connection (high side of 1's 2 wing) and Fostering Team Play (high side of the 1's 7 security arrow) in the Relationship hemisphere. When the Enneatype 1 is able to quiet their inner critic, they can then play in the land of 7 (reducing the perception of and need for perfection). "Folding the taco" from Perfection over the equator line lands 1s in Decisiveness (high side of 1) and Achieves Results. When making decisions, using their superpower of discernment, this reminds 1s to also take into consideration the Caring Connection component diagonally across, so that their decision isn't just task-based, but also takes into account human and relationship implications. Keep in mind that Perfection and Critical may not be the only behavior attributes that may be perceived as high in Enneatype 1s. Their need to be right, coupled with their mindset that they know what is right in any situation, may also be experienced by others as Arrogance, so that Leadership Circle Profile score may be elevated as well. Arrogance can be mitigated through movement to the 1's 9 wing into Community Concern and Sustainable Productivity. Sometimes, the motivation to be perfect and do the right thing may also be construed as Autocratic (where the 1s are always telling people what needs to be done and how to do it better) or Ambition (where they seek leadership positions so that they have the authority to do so). In these cases, 1's development focus to movement to the high side of its 9 wing, in the Relationship space of Selfless Leader, Balance, and Composure, may be the perfect antidote.

Enneatype 2s tend to score high in Pleasing and Arrogance in the Reactive hemisphere. The diagonal development pathway for 2s from the Reactive Relationship quadrant to the Creative Task quadrant lands them in the Purposeful & Visionary (high side of the 2's 8 stress arrow) and Achieves Results (high side of the 2's 3 wing) sectors. By applying this filter to requests made of them, 2s can prioritize what to agree to (if it is something that is part of their remit and will help achieve their goals and strategy) or if it's something they can decline (or delegate or pass onto a more appropriate party). The journey then flips from Pleasing, across the equator line in the same Relationship quadrant, landing on Collaboration and Mentoring & Developing (both high sides of 2). This reminds 2s that they don't need to take everything on themselves, and instead can look to partner with others to fulfill a request, either through Collaboration with someone else who knows how to do this or by Mentoring & Developing someone else who can continue to respond to an on-going request in the future. Arrogance can come into play when Enneatype 2s take pride in intuitively knowing (or assuming that they know) what other people need and/or when they take on too much themselves, because no one else can do it (better), especially when the 1 and 3 wings start to exert their influence. This tendency can be mitigated by reminding 2s to take the journey diagonally across from Arrogance (sometimes also associated with the 2's Enneatype 8 stress arrow) to Personal Learner (the 8's security integration arrow), involving asking questions of others to gain an understanding of the full picture.

Enneatype 3s tend to score high in Driven and Ambition in the Reactive hemisphere. "Folding the taco" within the Task hemisphere lands them in the Purposeful & Visionary and Strategic Focus (3's "eyes on the prize" orientation) and Systems Thinking and Sustainable Productivity (high side of 3's arrow to Enneatype 9) areas of the Creative hemisphere. Traversing diagonally from the Task to the Relationship hemisphere suggests that Balance, Composure, and Selfless Leader (3's arrow to the high side of 9), along with Interpersonal Intelligence, Collaboration, and Mentoring & Developing (3's 2 wing) could provide a means to mitigate the derailers associated with high Driven and Ambition, which can include burnout and burning bridges to achieve the goal,

The How and Why: Taking Care of Business With The Enneagram

no matter what. The Creative space encourages Enneatype 3s to remove their ego and identification with their successes from the equation, and instead shift focus to the good of the team and/or enterprise.

The sample size of Enneatype 4s in corporate settings is pretty sparse, so there is very limited data on which to report out. It can be safely concluded, however, that there is a tendency for Distance (given their more introverted, internal-referencing tendencies), counteracted by their Courageous Authenticity (high side of 1, 4, and 8). If overdone, their Courageous Authenticity may come off as Critical, straddling both Task and Relationship worlds in the Reactive hemisphere, so these Leadership Circle Profile scores may be high as well. They can be counteracted through focus on positive and constructive reframes to stay within the high side of Courageous Authenticity, directly across from Critical in the Creative space. 4's Integrity scores tend to be high as well, as Enneatype 4s value genuineness and authenticity. The corporate sector could benefit from more Enneatype 4 energy, harnessing their constellation of Creative gifts, which also includes actual creativity, not specifically called out or measured in the Leadership Circle as a distinct behavior.

Enneatype 5s tend to score high in Distance and Arrogance in the Reactive hemisphere. Note that Arrogance is also affiliated with the low side of Enneatype 8, and 5's natural security arrow integration. It is easy to see the path from the Arrogance in the Reactive Task quadrant to the Personal Learner in the Creative Relationship quadrant (the high side of 5), where Enneatype 5s can explore asking questions to find out more about people and situations rather than assuming superior knowledge about them. Staying within the Task hemisphere, another pathway to reduce Arrogance is Courageous Authenticity (the high side of 5's movement to its 8 arrow in security) and Community Concern (a nod to the 8's 9 wing and 5's 6 wing). In this way, Enneatype 5s are invited to consider external factors, resources, and consequences in addition to their default personal insights. Distance contributes to Enneatype 5s' superpower of objectivity and creates the environment enabling their inherent gifts in data analysis, pattern identification, and sense-making. Too much distance, however, can lead to perceptions of disinterest, disengagement, and even Arrogance. These can be countered through the same connections already mentioned when working on reducing Arrogance: this time it's a diagonal traversal from the Reactive Relational quadrant to Courageous Authenticity (5's movement to the high side of 8, 5's integration arrow to security) and Community Concern (5's 6 wing) in the Creative Task quadrant. Personal Learner and Composure are the high sides of 5, and are exactly where we land when "folding the taco" from Distance within the Relationship hemisphere. Thus, 5s can leverage their investigative curiosity to emphasize their engagement and interest, and reduce perceptions of Distance.

Enneatype 6s tend to score high in Conservative and Belonging in the Reactive hemisphere. This makes sense due to the 6 yearning for a tribal affiliation and risk-aversion (at least in the non-counter phobic subtypes!) for comfort, safety, and security. It can make sense for 6s to take the diagonal journey from Conservative in the Reactive Relationship quadrant to the Creative Task quadrant and land on Achieves Results and Decisiveness (the high sides of 6's movement to its stress arrow point of 3). Additional insights can be cultivated from 6's "folding the taco" just over the equator line, landing on Caring Connection (the high side of 6 in fitting into the tribe) and Fosters Team Play (6's 7 wing). Launching from the Belonging category in the Reactive Relationship quadrant, 6s can travel diagonally into the Creative Task quadrant, landing on Systems Thinking (6's movement to its security arrow 9 point) and Strategic Focus (6's movement to its stress arrow 3 point and 7 wing). These Creative behaviors can help the 6s take a bigger picture perspective, focusing on more positive opportunities and possibilities rather than fixating on worst-case scenarios and needs for safety. Staying within the boundaries of the Relationship hemisphere, "flipping the taco" from Belonging lands the 6 in Interpersonal Intelligence and Selfless Leader, high points of 6's movement to its stress point of 3 and comfort point of 9, respectively. Here, 6s can leverage the insights of their hearts and guts/bodies to get out of the anxieties and self-doubts in their heads.

Enneatype 7s tend to score high in Pleasing in the Reactive hemisphere. This can be attributed to their positive outlook, enthusiasm, and reluctance to say no to new opportunities for fear of missing out. A diagonal journey from the Reactive Relationship quadrant to the Creative Task quadrant lands 7s in the behaviors of Purposeful & Visionary (high side of 7) and Achieves Results (high side of 7's movement to its 1 stress point). This can help 7s focus on the right activities and goals in the attainment of the right results. Being part of the assertiveness triad that has no issues with asking for what they want (Enneatypes 3, 7, and 8), Enneatype 7s may also land some high scores in Arrogance, Autocratic, Ambition, and Driven. As we've seen with Enneatype 5s (and will see with Enneatype 8s), Arrogance can be tempered by "flipping the taco" to Personal Learner, where 7s can access their 5 security arrow point to slow down to ask questions, rather than assume they know and speed on through. Ambition and Drive can be mitigated by "folding the taco" within the Task hemisphere to the 7's natural high side of Systems Thinking and Strategic Focus and Purposeful & Visionary. Focusing on these tactics can help oust the ego from the 7s' Reactive patterns and focus more in the Creative space where the bigger picture takes precedence.

Enneatype 8s tend to score high in Arrogance and Autocratic in the Reactive hemisphere. This aligns with 8s' tendency to be direct, decisive, action-oriented, and powerful/power-driven. To escape the entrapments and possible derailers associated with these tendencies, 8s can traverse from Arrogance in the Reactive Task quadrant to Community Concern and Sustainable Productivity (components of 8's 9 wing) in the Creative Task quadrant. As we've seen above, the negative effects of Arrogance can be diminished by traveling diagonally to Personal Learner (8's movement to its 5 stress arrow point) in the Creative Relationship quadrant. Asking questions to understand, rather than directing dictatorially will help to reduce perceptions of Arrogance. Autocratic can be further reduced through the neighboring behaviors of Composure, Balance, and Selfless Leader, all three representing the 8's 9 wing qualities. 8's work to dial down their intensity and energy will support success in this area. Enneatypes 8s can also receive high Critical scores in the Reactive space, especially due to their propensity for speaking up and debating to get to truth. These can be tempered by working on their natural strengths in the high side of 8 of Integrity and Courageous Authenticity, directly across the circle when "folding the taco."

Enneatype 9s tend to score high in Passive and Pleasing in the Reactive hemisphere. High Passive can be interpreted by others as 9s being disinterested or disengaged in the work or relationship. It can be counteracted by 9s taking the journey and "folding the taco" from Passive in the Reactive Relationship quadrant to Sustainable Productivity and Community Concern (the high sides of 9 and 9's movement to its 3 security arrow) in the Creative Task quadrant. A jaunt contained within the Relationship hemisphere lands us in the Composure and Balance behaviors (both comprising the high side of 9). By leveraging their natural attention on the community/environment and its welfare, and tapping into their focus on sustainability with regard to productivity and effectiveness, 9s can counter the perception that they are not engaged or interested. Their innate prowess in Composure and Balance can also be leveraged to temper any Passive tendencies. From the Pleasing dimension, 9s can follow the same journey as 2s and 7s: "Folding the taco" from the Reactive Relationship quadrant to the Creative Task quadrant lands 9s in the Strategic Focus (high side of 9's movement to its security arrow of 3, which also includes Achieves Results) and Purposeful & Visionary (high side of 9 and 8 wing) realms. These qualities can help 9s prioritize where to focus their energies to be more sustainably successful. To do this, they can also leverage their natural strengths in Collaboration and Mentoring and Developing others, so they don't have to go it alone.

It is also important to keep in mind that each of the Reactive tendencies has positive attributes associated with it. If they are used appropriately and consciously, they can be beneficial. If they are overused, they can become potential career derailers.

Enneatype 1's Perfection is important for attentiveness to quality results, but can become debilitating if it prevents action or decisiveness while waiting for the ever-elusive and unattainable state of perfection. Enneatype 1's Critical is

The How and Why: Taking Care of Business With The Enneagram

important in critical thinking and improvement, but can become divisive if used to constantly criticize others without any constructive and productive proposals for solutions.

Enneatype 2, 7, and 9's Pleasing is important in relationship-building and nurturing, but can actually hinder relationship trust when promises can't be kept due to overcommitment.

Enneatype 3's Drive and Ambition plays a huge role in motivating advancement and achievement of success, but can become a derailer if one is perceived as too ambitious and leaves a trail of dead bodies in their wake.

Enneatype 5's Distance helps their objectivity, while the gift of Arrogance is self-confidence. If over-relied upon and overused, however, Distance can be perceived as unattachment and disinterest and Arrogance becomes, well, ugly, off-putting, and demotivating arrogance.

Enneatype 6's Conservativeness supports rule following and safety. Overused it can prevent innovation, creativity, and forward motion.

The gift of Enneatype 8's Arrogance is in self-confidence. However, too much self-confidence can lead to others experiencing 8s as arrogant. The gift of Autocratic is the ability to take authority and control and provide direction. This is important in certain situations (when people need direction if they are novices in a certain area or during crises/emergencies), but it can become tiresome and demotivating in everyday operations.

The gift of Passive for Enneatype 9s is from the opportunity to provide space for others to think, problem-solve, think, and make decisions on their own, as opposed to providing the solution for them. On the other end of the spectrum, too much space may be interpreted by others as 9s being disengaged, disinterested, or even invisible.

The role of culture and some other general observations

Self-Preservation Enneagram subtypes (or those who tend to use Self-Preservation in their top two Subtype stacking) tend to have higher scores in Distance, a reflection of introversion, regardless of primary Enneagram type. Furthermore, regardless of one's primary Enneagram type affiliation, we can also expect to see some other patterns play out that can be related to a person's tri-type/triadic style (the styles they use to access their thinking, feeling, and action/gut centers). Company and culture overlays can also show up in a person's LCP, and should be taken into consideration in coaching.

Country culture (or culture of upbringing) can play a huge role in overlays of behaviors and motivations. This creates an added element of complexity and robustness to human beings, and can many times be reflected in unexpected spikes of scores on the Leadership Circle Profile, which may at first blush seem to indicate a client's core motivation, but may not be so. For example, I have noticed a trend where my Canadian clients seem to be scored relatively high in Passive by their (also Canadian) raters. Knowing this can help a coach dig deeper to determine what the real, underlying issue and motivation may be – the core issue to be focused on that will yield transformational change, rather than a symptom that may only be an indicator of cultural projection.

Company culture is also an important, yet sometimes deceptive, factor when coaches try to help their clients to identify their core motivations. Companies advertise their values and principles overtly and in their business practices. This leads them to attract and reward (read: promote) people who align and represent these values and principles through their explicit behaviors. This culture is fortified further as these leaders then hire in their own images, via myriad unconscious biases. We then end up with a leadership phenotype which keeps propagating itself throughout the organization until a new senior leadership phenotype emerges, takes hold, and cascades. We see certain patterns emerge because of this, with organizations displaying and promulgating a definitive core Enneagram type, manifesting as certain Leadership Circle Creative behaviors and Reactive tendencies on the LCP. The LCP high scores and related core type, is based on the Enneagram core, tri-types/triadic styles, wings, secondary, tertiary, and other Enneagram points available to their employees, since we all have inherent access to multiple Enneagram points within us, regardless of our core affiliation. When these are aggregated, a dominant and common Enneatype emerges, reflected in high scores in their related LCP categories.

Thus, awareness of an organization's cultural and leadership phenotype is imperative in effectively coaching its people, especially when it comes to validating whether the presenting high scores in certain LCP categories are due to the company's culture or the individual's true core motivations. These insights can help coaches in working with their clients to explain any employees' lack of culture fit, confusion around what "executive presence" means in this setting, developing precautions against groupthink, and finding ways to mine and harness diversity of perspective. Knowledge of the company's culture also allows coaches to hold that construct separately, while helping their clients investigate what other motivations may also be guiding their mindsets and behaviors – and what development will be most appropriate, meaningful, productive, and transformative for them given their environmental situation.

The Leadership Circle Profile is a very powerful tool that provides users with a map to help them understand their stuff – their strengths, potential derailers, and development journeys. Knowledge of the Enneagram enhances the understanding of this framework (since the Enneagram was embedded in its creation) and development pathways inherent in its structure. Fortuitously, the Full Circle Group, which created the Leadership Circle Profile, has also conducted research into its effectiveness. Their findings indicate that there is validity in its construct and shows that those with greater access to the Creative behaviors (which reflect the high points of each Enneagram type) tend to be associated with better leadership and more successful organizations. Extending the transitive property, we can therefore also see

The How and Why: Taking Care of Business With The Enneagram

the Enneagram's relevance in contributing to leadership excellence and business success. Used in tandem, these tools provide a way to truly help people transform themselves and their organizations for the better.

Chapter 11

Team-Building

Organization Development consultants and Human Resources practitioners use myriad tools and products within organizations to help bring teams together and work more effectively together. These include the ubiquitous Myers-Briggs Type Instrument (MBTI), DiSC, StrengthsFinder, and many other variants that take these standards and add their signature stamp to them by changing the nomenclature. The Enneagram is not always the best tool to use for team-building events, especially since they tend to be just that: one-time events. Plus, the Enneagram is a very intricate, multi-layered development framework that can take up to a lifetime (if ever!) to fully comprehend. However, when a team commits to consciously using and integrating the Enneagram framework in their day-to-day interactions and business processes, they become far more effective and successful.

A tried-and-proven way to introduce the Enneagram to teams for the purpose of team development is in tandem with other, more familiar instruments. This works especially well since these self-assessment standards are very well correlated with the Enneagram. For example, I recommend a series

The How and Why: Taking Care of Business With The Enneagram

of DiSC, MBTI, followed by the Enneagram (check out Appendix C to see their interrelationships and correlations). It's a natural progression since DiSC has only four, easy-to-understand dimensions (Dominance, Influence, Steadiness, and Conscientiousness) and very naturally makes the point about individual differences, preferences, and default operating systems. This helps drive the lesson about self-awareness and its relation to empathy for others with different perspectives and needs. Recall our discussion of this system's use in Chapter 9 on Communication. MBTI also has just four dimensions: How one re-energizes, how one prefers to take in information, what genre of criteria one uses to make decisions, and how one prefers to relate to time, schedules, and need for closure. Once workshop attendees become familiar with the relatively easy-to-comprehend MBTI, they begin to realize that there are sixteen variations of personality type. This, too, supports the previous learning involving the Platinum Rule requiring self-awareness and empathy for others. In addition, they realize that DiSC and MBTI can only explain some limited elements of personality, especially if they have teammates with the same DiSC and MBTI styles who are very different from each other. Then it becomes easy and natural to introduce the Enneagram as yet another tool to explain some of the variances that DiSC and MBTI cannot. We have already discussed how DiSC relates to the Enneagram in Chapter 9. Here is how the Enneagram and the MBTI correlate:

STUDY/ ENNEATYPE	PALMER (1988)	WAGNER (1990)	O'LEARY (1990)	HAVENS (1995)	HEBENSTREIT (2007)	CHERNICK-FAUVRE (2015)
1	I-T-	---J	-S-J	E-TJ	----	ISTJ
2	E---	--F-	--F-	E-FJ	--F-	ENFJ
3	E---	E--J	E---	E-FJ	----	ENFJ
4	--F-	-NFP	INFP	I-FJ	--F-	INFP
5	I-T-	I-T-	INT-	I-TJ	I-T-	INTP
6	INT-	I-F-	IS-J	I-TJ	----	ISFJ
7	ENT-	EN--	EN-P	E-FP	----	ENTP
8	ENT-	EN--	E--P	E-TJ	E---	ENTJ
9	I---	----	-S--	I-FP	----	ISFP

(Adapted from Havens, 1995, p. 28)

Figure 11-1 | Myers-Briggs Type Instrument and Enneagram Correlates

Note that Katherine Chernick-Fauvre's results reflect tendencies she has observed in collecting data from over 1,000 of her respondents, some of which were statistically significant, while others were less so.

Knowledge of the correlations between Enneagram and Myers-Briggs types can help Enneagram novices in identifying, validating, and understanding their true type.

PRACTITIONER NOTE

The use of animals can also help Enneagram novices get a faster grasp of the Enneagram typology. A fun way to end an Introductory Enneagram workshop is to have the participants identify which animal relates to which Enneagram Type and why. Practitioners can do this with stuffed animal

The How and Why: Taking Care of Business With The Enneagram

representations or with pictures projected on a screen. Depending on the audience, this closing exercise can also be conducted with toy cars.

ENNEATYPE	ANIMAL CORRELATE(S)	VEHICLE CORRELATE(S)
1	Ant, Dragon	Lexus
2	Dog	Ambulance, Tow Truck
3	Fox, Octopus	BMW, Corvette
4	Donkey, Horse, Unicorn	1920s-1950s Roadsters
5	Owl	Honda CRV/HRV, News Van
6	Rabbit, Cat	Volvo
7	Hummingbird, Monkey	Jeep Wrangler
8	Lion	Hummer, Tank
9	Elephant, Sheep, Cow	Trailer, Train Caboose

Figure 11-2 | Animals and Vehicles Correlated to the Enneagram

Here is some of the reasoning behind these exemplars:

- Ants and Dragons have Enneatype 1 tendencies in that Ants are very diligent, focused, and meticulous in their tasks. Dragons are considered the "perfect" creature in Asian culture. Lexus's past advertising slogan has been "The relentless pursuit of perfection."
- Dogs, especially companion canines, are considered excellent representatives of the Enneatype 2's intuitiveness and helpfulness. Ambulances and tow trucks can also reflect this helpful nature.
- Foxes are very clever in doing whatever it takes to achieve their goal. Octopi are also great symbols of Enneatype 3 due to their ability to morph themselves (change colors) to adapt to whatever the situation calls for, along with using their multiple extensions to multitask! The performance and image aspects of Enneatype 3 can be referenced in

high-status, high-performance vehicles like the Corvette and BMW.
- The uniqueness, sadness, and beauty of Enneatype 4 can be seen, respectively, in unicorns, donkeys (think Eeyore), and horses. Their retrospective nature of longing for the past can be recalled in classic, dramatic "fender-tastic" vehicles of days gone by.
- The owl is an easy choice to represent the knowledge-seeking Enneatype 5. Their unobtrusive nature can be played out by choosing subdued, practical vehicles that blend in, like the not-too-flashy Honda CR-V. We can humorously extend the information-seeking metaphor by also including a news van, with its satellite dishes and antennas, into this mix.
- The curious and skittish nature of cats and rabbits can serve as a reflection of Enneatype 6. With Volvo's reputation and focus on safety, we can easily make the connection to Enneatype 6 here, as well.
- Hummingbirds are fast-moving and flit from one flower or birdfeeder to another. Monkeys present a generally carefree and fun-loving nature. Both can be used as symbols for Enneatype 7. And since Jeep Wranglers are touted as being the ultimate adventure vehicles, it makes sense that they would appeal to the Enneatype 7.
- The lion is the king of the jungle. It is a symbol of power and authority, much like the attributes of the Enneatype 8. These qualities can also be associated with the aggressive, imposing, dominating, powerful, and indestructible image presented by the Hummer or a tank.
- Elephants, sheep, and cows emote a certain quiet, peaceful nature. They tend to "go with the flow" and generally do not "rock the boat." The elephant also has an immovable connotation to it, sometimes also attributed to Enneatype 9. Provocative and potentially humorous vehicle depictions that can apply to 9s include towable trailers or train

The How and Why: Taking Care of Business With The Enneagram

cabooses, since they tag along to another vehicle that is providing the power and direction.

Rather than being dogmatic about the absolute correctness of the above (admittedly and blatantly stereotypical) connections, encourage the group to talk about the reasons they have in choosing their selections. This is meant as a lighthearted way to end a workshop with a quick discussion to check the group's understanding of the nuances of each Enneatype, not necessarily a pass/fail final exam. Note, too, that there are other interpretations and variations on which animals are representative of the Enneagram styles. Rohr and Ebert (2001) allocate them as follows:

Enneatype 1: Terrier, Ant, Bee
Enneatype 2: Cat, Donkey, Puppy
Enneatype 3: Chameleon, Peacock, Eagle
Enneatype 4: Mourning Dove, Basset Hound, Oyster
Enneatype 5: Owl, Fox, Hamster
Enneatype 6: Rabbit, Wolf, German Shepherd, Rat
Enneatype 7: Monkey, Butterfly
Enneatype 8: Rhinoceros, Rattlesnake, Tiger, Bull
Enneatype 9: Elephant, Sloth, Whale, Dolphin

A practical "take-away" for the team is a cheat sheet of sorts that can help each team member to recall each Enneatype's strengths, how to use their clockwise wing for growth and development, and their hot buttons/drainers/pet peeves – so that team members can avoid pushing them.

ENNEATYPE	STRENGTH	LEARN FROM WING	HOT BUTTON
1	Discernment, focus on excellence	2: Consider impact on people & relationships	Go against their values/morals
2	Intuition about others' needs	3: Focus on results, not just relationships	Not being appreciated for their help
3	Goal-achievement	4: Slow down; Stop and smell the roses	Blocked goal attainment; tarnished reputation
4	Empathy, Passion	5: Compartmentalize/ control feelings	Made to feel not special or unique
5	Objectivity, Sense-making	6: Plan-making	Irrational change/ break in routine; spotlight
6	Contingency planning	7: Positive options	Disloyalty/ loss of trust; threat to comfort, safety, security
7	Positivity, vision, ideas and possibilities	8: Execute on ideas	Limits; Rules
8	Execution (through others)	9: Dial back high energy; Diplomacy and peace-making	Injustice; Harm to inner circle or turf
9	Systemic view; value of everything	1: Differentiation and decision-making	Conflict; Change; Disturbance to the status quo

Figure 11-3 | Team Enneagram Type Strengths, Growth, and Hot Buttons

After determining the Enneagram type of individuals on a team, it can be very powerful to plot the types of the individuals within teams to predict potential and address current conflict.

The How and Why: Taking Care of Business With The Enneagram

Understanding a leader's style in comparison to his/her team can also reveal where the team may butt heads or fall victim to groupthink. Pay attention to the team's Harmonic Styles. Sum up how many team members are in each of the Harmonic Triads to see where the majority reside. If the majority of the team is comprised of Enneatypes 2, 7, and 9 – the Positive Outlook Triad – the team is very likely to avoid or try to escape conflict. An abundance of Enneatypes 1, 3, and 5 – the Competency Triad – will compartmentalize their feelings and dive into objective and logical problem resolution. A plurality of Enneatypes 4, 6, and 8 – the Reactive Triad - will respond strongly and emotionally to conflict and need to know about other peoples' support and commitment. Share these tendencies with the team so that they know how they are likely to respond to conflict. Lead them in a conversation about how they can optimize their response to conflict to make it more productive.

When bringing together team members for an Organization Development intervention on team-building, it will become necessary to call out and remind them of the stage within the normal evolution of team development in which they're currently engaged, any through which they may have already passed, and what phases are in store for them. When they get to an actual team-building intervention, the team will most likely be somewhere in the Storming to Norming phases of Tuckman's Model of Team Development. I like to overlay the Situational Leadership model in these conversations, since this plan of action intended for individuals can also be applied to working with teams. And we can also show how the Enneagram comes into play in both these systems:

The Enneagram, Situational Leadership, and the Tuckman Model of Team Development

The Tuckman Model of Team Development defines the evolution of a team progressing through the stages of Forming, Storming, Norming, and, finally, Performing. The Adjourning phase can also be added to this, in cases where the team is disbanded upon the project's successful completion. Let's look at what happens at each phase:

Forming is a time of excitement and optimism. The members of the teams are usually excited by being asked to be part of a new venture and the possibilities this may bring. This relates well to the Positive Outlook Triad of 2, 7, and 9. If we overlay the Situational Leadership model here (which prescribes that individuals at this entry phase of development require more high touch care, attention, and direction), we can see the directive leadership qualities of Enneatypes 8 and 1 being required for successful navigation of this phase and evolution to the next.

The honeymoon is now over. The initial excitement over the new project has waned. Team members are feeling disgruntled and frustrated. Things are not turning out the way they imagined they would. There's lots of jockeying for power by multiple team members. There's discord. Fighting. Conflict abounds. We're now in the throes of

The How and Why: Taking Care of Business With The Enneagram

the Storming phase of team development. Characteristics of Enneatypes 8 (debate, striving to gain power and claim and exert authority), 6 (questioning, skepticism, contingency planning), and 5 (seeking more data and knowledge about the situation) are evident. The Situational Leadership Model prescribes a coaching style consisting of high directive and high supportive behaviors (Enneatype 2 strengths) at this stage in order to progress to the next one.

The Norming phase is the most likely stage that assistance from an Organization Development practitioner will be sought. And the continuous support (as prescribed by the Situational Leadership model) related to the Enneatype 2 will come in very handy here. Norming requires the identification of, and agreement to, explicit rules of engagement. How will the team members work with each other to accomplish the team's goals? Remember that what differentiates a team from a group is the interdependency of the members in relying and depending on each other to be successful. This needs to be fully understood by all team members. And they all need to agree to and abide by the norms and principles that will get them there. The qualities of Enneatypes 1 (rules, order) and 4 (empathy, meaning) are called for here. And they are both arrows of the supportive Enneatype 2.

Once the norms are developed, communicated, and espoused by all team members, the stage is set for the team to become high-performing. A definite Enneatype 3 quality. At this point, the low directive and low supportive modes of delegating and execution (qualities associated with Enneatype

8) will come into play to keep the project moving forward and in balance (an Enneatype 9 quality). Keep in mind, though, that this balance may be upset at any time with the introduction or departure of a team member. Should that occur, the team will regress to a previous phase and need to work through it all over again in order to progress through the next stages to the elusive "high performance" apex once more.

It is fascinating to note how similar the team development model is to the strategic planning process, discussed in Chapter 4. Note how this, too, starts at 7, goes to 6 and 5, then 1 and 4, then 3 and ends at 8/9. Interesting how that works out, isn't it?

Other clever uses of the Enneagram to enhance team development have been successfully developed and deployed by several practitioners.

The 9 Domains Framework allows one to assess the general health of a team, or organization, in terms of the Enneagram:
1. Self-Regulation & Organization, Integrity (Honesty, fairness, impeccability, wisdom, impartiality, discernment, conscientiousness, congruence, truthfulness, purpose)
2. Nurture & Connection, Service (Nurture and self-nurture, unselfishness, empathy, attunement to others, concern, appreciation, encouragement)
3. Self-Development & Adaptability (Inner direction, modesty, self-acceptance, authenticity, self-assurance, admirability, poise, accomplishment, focus)
4. Self-Repair & Individuality, Self-Development

(Introspection, self-awareness, intuition, sensitivity, self-honesty, discretion, emotional strength, meaningfulness)
5. Intelligence & Contextual Awareness, Knowledge (Profundity, curiosity, pioneering, insightfulness, objectivity, perceptiveness, originality, inventiveness)
6. Internal Support & Interdependence, Mutual Support (Grounded-ness, interdependence, fortitude, reliability, preparedness, faithfulness, devotion, mutuality)
7. Energy & Openness to Change (Appreciation, receptivity, satisfaction, joyfulness, enthusiasm, resilience, vivaciousness, productivity, versatility)
8. Expansion & Forward, Decisive Action (Courage, self-surrender, majesty, self-confidence, strength, action-orientation, empowerment, protectiveness)
9. Balance & Dynamic Stability (Self-possession, serenity, presence, peacefulness, flow, naturalness, optimism, humility, inclusivity, patience)

Facilitating a conversation around these areas in the Norming phase of team development can help guide the team members in creating a set of robust and all-inclusive operating guidelines and rules of engagement that will help the team be successful. This set of principles can also be applied in an "after action review" (also referred to as a retrospective, or more morbidly called a "post mortem") where, after the project has been completed, the team members convene to review how the process went and what lessons were learned that can be applied to future similar projects.

Some items that may come out of an after action review

may relate to the same major challenges that any and all teams face and must overcome, regardless of industry, sector, or company size. Patrick Lencioni calls them out in his best-selling tome, *The Five Dysfunctions of a Team*:

- Absence of Trust
- Fear of Conflict
- Lack of Commitment
- Avoidance of Accountability
- Inattention to Results

Note how these relate so well to the Enneagram type strengths. Enneagram 6s search for trust and then become loyal to a proven trustworthy organization or leader. Fear of conflict can be flipped around to the strengths of the Enneagram 8s, who eagerly engage in conflict to find the truth in the situation or use debate to get the best result. Commitment-phobia is a stereotypical 7 trait, which is also related to the avoidance of accountability. This can easily be harnessed in the strengths of the Enneagram Type 1. Inattention to results can be counteracted by the Enneagram 3s laser-like focus on them. Tapping into the strengths of team members, who embody the positive aspects of the dysfunctions, can help turn dysfunctional teams into high-performing teams. It also highlights the need for diversity of perspectives and motivations in teams so that we can avoid the formation of like-minded, group think-oriented teams which become dysfunctional in their myopia and produce poor products, services, and results.

The How and Why: Taking Care of Business With The Enneagram

Building trust in teams is dependent on team members being able to rely on their fellow team members keeping their word, and is enhanced by each person being open and vulnerable with each other. A way to achieve vulnerability and openness is through sharing deeply personal insights. Since everyone is a compilation of all Enneagram styles, the exercise below can be used in team meetings where each team member takes a turn at responding to a specific sentence completion (this process can be spread out over multiple meetings, perhaps as an icebreaker):

1. The value(s) that I hold most dearly that is/are currently being threatened or compromised is/are ...
2. The connection(s) that I hold most dearly that is/are currently being threatened or compromised is/are ... The support that I really need from others right now is ...
3. The competence that I want to be known for is ... The failures of which I am most afraid right now are ...
4. Where I am most being taken for granted is ... I feel like I am not being seen when ...
5. What I am withholding is ...
6. My biggest fear is ...
7. Where I'm afraid I'll have no choice is ... I'm afraid of saying "no" to ...
8. I feel most vulnerable when ...
9. Where I am resisting or delaying taking action is ...

As each team member provides his/her answer to these sentence completions, regardless of Enneagram type, and depending on how self-aware and ready team members are to share their truths, the conditions will be set for trust on the team to develop more strongly.

PRACTITIONER NOTE

Here is another very practical and positive way to kick off a meeting, workshop, or off-site. This is especially effective when this is the first time working with the team and/or if it's a new team coming together for a team-building or strategic planning session.

This exercise is a powerful way to get team members to identify and call out the positive attributes of their coworkers. It is especially useful when used with a new leader, providing valuable insight into how other team members see each other (which may counteract the leader's initial impressions) and understanding about how and why each individual came to the field/discipline and company (and how the leader can motivate them appropriately). A glimpse into a person's Enneagram style will often be manifested during this positive, appreciative inquiry-esque exercise. And it is much better received than the traditional and tired "two truths and a lie" or "tell us something no one else knows" icebreakers.

If team size causes concern due to time constraints that could prevent running this icebreaker in its totality, an abbreviated, yet equally impactful version of this exercise can be used. This varietal works especially well when there are new team members who can benefit from learning a quick introduction to the value that each of the existing team members brings. Ask for a volunteer from the team and have him/her select someone else on the team who s/he knows very well. The task is for the volunteer to introduce this other team member to the newbies by sharing with everyone that team member's unique skills, strengths, and special value that s/he adds to the team. Once that introduction is complete, and the target is sufficiently appreciated and humbled, the targeted team member then selects a different team member to introduce to the newbies using the same formula. Repeat the process until all team members have been introduced and honored, and the final team member introduces the first volunteer who started the exercise.

This icebreaker exercise is always very well-received, as participants see its immediate applicability in a variety of business settings and have even referred to it as "an adult icebreaker!" Coupled with insights from the Enneagram, it can become even more meaningful and powerful. It's also a great way for a meeting moderator/facilitator to introduce him/herself to a new group or team and gain immediate credibility without coming off as pompous or arrogant. Lastly, it provides a great bridge to strategic planning or mission statement work that the facilitator may be leading later on in the day. This adult icebreaker works as a precursor to any meeting.

Inform the meeting participants that their first group exercise is to create their personal mission statement. Model to them what it will look like by introducing yourself with your prepared personal mission statement following the formula below:

"Hello, my name is (your name). I am a (discipline/role/field) professional with (quantity) years of experience in the (name of industries or sectors) industries. My strengths include (list your functional/technical strengths associated with success in your field/discipline/role). I am particularly adept at (list some general strengths and interpersonal success factors). I do this because (call out your raison d'être)."

Give the group 5 – 10 minutes to create their individual personal mission statements with the following criteria:

- Designed to be delivered in 30 seconds or less (like an elevator pitch)
- Does not have to be final and perfect – in fact, participants are encouraged to copy ideas from one another (if they are applicable and true) and tailor them to fit and align with future situations and different audiences
- Should eventually be memorized to serve as a template that can be customized to fit any occasion

Depending on the number of participants and their familiarity with each other, select the best way for the round robin and debrief. If it's a relatively small group (less than a dozen people) who have worked with each other for at least 6 months, ask each person to read his/her personal mission statement out loud, one volunteer at a time. When the first person reads his/her personal mission statement, ask the rest of the group what s/he may have missed (or, if you're feeling comfortable enough with the group and want to be a little cheeky, "What did they overstate?"). That also serves to break the ice with the group. To this date, no one has ever had to remove any of his/her stated strengths from his/her personal mission statement! As more and more positive attributes are brought forth, make sure the volunteer writes them down and incorporates them into his/her personal mission statement. Inevitably, someone will not automatically write down the additional input; you may wish to call out that behavior in a fun way by saying something along the lines of: "At least pretend to write it down so your coworker won't feel bad!" Keep asking the group "What else?" to generate as much input as possible and then ask the volunteer how s/he feels about the input. To provide closure and move onto the next volunteer, lead the group in a round of applause after each speaker's turn.

After all participants have taken their turn at reading their personal

The How and Why: Taking Care of Business With The Enneagram

mission statements, received additional positive input from their coworkers to incorporate into it, been asked how they feel, and received their applause for their bravery, ask the group "Where and when do you see yourself being able to use your personal mission statement?"

Tease out these answers if they don't naturally come out from the group:
- During an interview, when the interviewee is asked "Tell me about yourself"
- On a résumé, as a Summary of Qualifications
- Note: If you are working with an intact team within an organization, be sure to add that this is no way implies that the company is encouraging people to look for work outside the organization!
- On a LinkedIn profile
- On customer visits, where employees need to introduce themselves to the client
- When meeting new employees and coworkers
- At professional association networking events
- When asked by an executive on an elevator (that's why it needs to be deliverable within 30 seconds)
- When introducing oneself to a candidate during an interview

If you are working with a larger group of people and have time constraints, a way to shorten this exercise is to have people share their personal mission statements and get feedback from table groups of 4 – 6 people. Then ask for only a few volunteers to share their personal mission statements with members of the larger group, from whom they will also receive feedback. This alternative is less effective than the previously-described approach and dissipates personal responsibility to do the work in the subgroups; it is not recommended unless you have the luxury of multiple facilitators able to monitor, assist, and keep the table groups on task.

A PRACTICAL APPLICATION

A team leader brought her new leadership team of 18 together for an off-site to:
- Conduct some team-building
- Determine how best to work and move forward in accomplishing their division's goals
- Discuss what has worked and identify areas of improvement in their on-going collaboration

We decided to use the Enneagram as the instrument for team-building. The team members took an online assessment a week before the scheduled off-site. The results revealed that the majority (almost 60%) were either Enneagram Type 3 or 8. This was not surprising for this innovative, start-up mentality biotechnology division. In addition, there was a strong preponderance (again, almost 60%) of Self-Preservation subtypes. This is good data for the facilitator to have in advance, so that s/he can plan how to structure the day most effectively. In this example, because of the high population of Self-Preservation subtypes (indicating Introversion), it made it even more important to send each team member his/her report in advance, so that s/he had the opportunity to peruse it before discussing it in a public setting. The multitude of Self-Preservation subtypes necessitated the need to ensure that the class participants:
- Felt safe in the process
- Were guaranteed that their report data would not be shared
- Were assured that their type would not be disclosed outside of the room without their express permission

The How and Why: Taking Care of Business With The Enneagram

Note: I lighten the mood around this topic by saying that no one is allowed to post any of these results to Facebook, Instagram, or Twitter! Along these lines, I also like to mention that any information they learn about the Enneagram types and their hot buttons can only be used for good and not for evil or manipulation, and ask them all to agree and commit to this.

Knowledge of the team's Self-Preservation/Introverted tendencies helped guide the set up the off-site by having advance communication of the discussion topics and about what the team members should come prepared to talk. That preparation paid off on the actual off-site day as everyone was excited and engaged throughout the process. Not surprisingly, a lot of the issues the team was experiencing revolved around intra-team and interpersonal conflict. The three top leaders happened to affiliate with Type 8 and were each very comfortable with conflict and debate. Not so much for the other 84% of the team. A healthy epiphany and outcome of the process was the development of "rules of engagement" for healthy and productive conflict and debate. They reached agreement for people to explicitly identify which "hat" or perspective they were about to wear (information-seeking, playing devil's advocate, corporate versus division versus functional). They came to a common understanding that the team would use these norms for the goal of extracting the best factual and objective information that would lead to the best decision.

The Enneagram is a very powerful tool to use in team-building. It can help team members to better understand themselves and each other, identify hot buttons to avoid, provide insight into how to motivate and persuade individuals, increase intra-team trust, and show how to effectively navigate the inevitable change and conflict that will come up. Its continued integration in these realms optimizes the chances of teams becoming high-performing rather than dysfunctional.

Chapter 12

Change Management

Change management is an ubiquitous need in and across all organizations. No company (or individual) can expect to keep doing the same thing and stay current and successful, given our constantly changing economic, technological, and political realms. Eduardo Torgal proposes using the Enneagram as a descriptor of the change management process. I have overlayed the Enneagram-Driven Strategic Planning Model (see Chapter 4) to provide even greater clarity and harmonization.

1. Everything is perfect! (Denial) – Enneatype 7 positivity
2. Bring in outside perspective/help to identify issues and what is needed to be addressed (Inform) – Enneatypes 5 and 6
3. Shock/Force/Resistance to change (Resistance) – Enneatypes 5 and 6
4. The realization that things really are bad and there is pain (Empathize) – Enneatype 4
5. Let it go! Let go of ourselves in resisting/blocking the change process (Exploration) – Enneatype 7
6. Creation of healthy doubt (Ask for Ideas) –

Enneatype 7
7. Define what we really want (Vision of the future and possibilities) – Enneatypes 7 and 1
8. Act on the new way (Accept) – Enneatypes 3 and 8
9. A new shock/revolution starts (Appreciate) – Enneatypes 2 and 9

In addition, the Enneagram provides change agents and facilitators with tools and insights into how to best approach different types in order to help them navigate and accept change, as effectively as possible. Elisabeth Kübler-Ross documents a grief management process that flows through Denial, Anger, Bargaining, Depression, and, finally, Acceptance. There are eerie similarities between the grief/loss process and the process through which people go when they encounter change: Denial, Resistance, Exploration, and, ultimately, Acceptance. Individuals go through this process at different rates and need to be supported and encouraged in different ways to optimize a healthy progression.

In the Denial phase, managers, coaches, and change agents need to emphasize consistent dissemination of information and knowledge. One can imagine how especially important this would be for Enneatypes 1, 5, and 6.

In the Resistance phase, empathy is in order. This would be especially meaningful for the heart types (2, 3, and 4).

In the Exploration phase, encouragement of options, alternatives, and other choices are encouraged. This would be especially true for Enneatypes 7, 8, and 9.

In the Acceptance stage, appreciation is in order. Everyone

needs appreciation, but wants to receive it in different ways.

Most, if not all, organization change management training programs focus on some version of the grief/loss cycle through which employees will progress at their own individual rates. They also stress the importance of constant and consistent communication from leadership, usually about what the change is going to entail and what the end state will look like. While this is definitely important, a critical component is overlooked: What additional information are employees looking for that is not being communicated? The Enneagram can provide insight into what to include in communications to help employees commit to the change faster. Their areas of concern should be addressed early on, in primary communications, instead of further on down the line, if at all. It will, therefore, be important for all change communications to address the following areas, as guided by the Enneagram:

Is this the right thing to do?
  Enneagram 1s are concerned about:
  - the ethics of a situation
  - that everyone will be treated equitably
  - that the change is in alignment with the values and mission of the organization.

How will it affect my work relationships? What about our customers and stakeholders?
  Enneagram 2s will want to know:

- how the change will impact their work relationships
- how will it affect internal and external customers and their experiences
- how will it affect their relationship with their leader
- how will their skillset and contributions be appreciated and valued in the new organizational structure

Does it support our goals? Is it the most efficient option? How will it affect my position? Title? Salary? Identity?

Enneagram 3s will be concerned about:
- what role they will have in the new structure
- whether their reputation will help them land a promotion
- if they will end up in a champion group

Will this change make my role and unique skillset redundant?

Enneagram 4s will want to know:
- how will their uniqueness be preserved and leveraged in the new world order

Is there data to support that this is the logical action to take?

Enneagram 5s will want to see:
- the research and already-proven best practices

Will this impact my job security?

Enneagram 6s will need to be:
- reassured that their jobs will be safe
- aligned with a (new) leader that they trust

The How and Why: Taking Care of Business With The Enneagram

Are there options for me to grow/explore in the new design?
Enneagram 7s will want to see:
- how this new change can create new and exciting opportunities for them to pursue and take advantage of
- that they will not be limited, stuck, or trapped

How will this affect my team and my department?
Enneagram 8s will be focused on:
- the impact to their power, authority, and span of control over their turf and people
- being reassured that their people will all be treated justly in the process and land well

How will this affect my current state of harmony? When will it be over?
Enneagram 9s are likely to be resistant to the change process that creates disequilibrium and want to:
- return to a state of status quo, as quickly and as painlessly as possible
- be reassured that everything will turn out OK

Change management and the progression of individuals through the change process mirrors the loss or death acceptance process. After all, change is really the end or death of a current state or situation. This is, hopefully, followed by the eventual acceptance and adoption of a new state or situation. The Enneagram can help us facilitate progress through this cycle, specific to Enneagram type.

	MOVES TOWARDS	MOVES AWAY FROM	DEFENSE MECHANISM & BEHAVIORAL MANIFESTATION	DEVELOPMENT PRACTICE
1	Purpose, mission Making a difference Calm, serenity Anger What is being said "can't be done" (a challenge)	Wrong, Unfairness Boredom Criticism Not being useful Feeling inadequate	Reaction formation (feeling one way, but behaving the opposite, i.e., acting as if all is fine even though feeling resentful or working tirelessly despite fatigue to satisfy the demands of the inner critic to be and do good).	Allow forgiveness. Recognize that there are many acceptable options, not just one right way. Stay friendly with the inner critic and avoid self-judgment while working through change. Engage in physical relaxation and indulgences, without trying to control everything. Allow loss of temper.
2	Inspiration/idealism Focusing on own needs (not others') Enhancing a positive / supportive / validating relationship Freedom Living a bigger, better, more self-expressive life Self-improvement / personal growth Taking advantage of new opportunities presented	Fleeing a bad situation/ relationship Burnout threshold experiences (the last straw)	Repression of personal needs and feelings to avoid being seen as needy and maintain image of being helpful, indispensable, needed. "You need me."	Spend time alone nurturing self and working through own feelings about the change. Take care of self before taking care of others and over-giving to them. Identify what is being repressed when anger arises. Be own person, not who others want/expect.
3	Approval Acknowledgment Efficiency The heart's desires Meaning, purpose Winning Search for goals	Chaos Being controlled Being embarrassed Under- or devalued Looking bad Failure Health crisis Identity	Over-identification with a specific role to avoid failure and maintain an image (to self and others) of success; Loss of true self to that image. Focus on tasks and goals to be achieved.	Slow down and allow/pay attention to feelings and their physical/bodily effects. Make everyday duties and chores playful and fun. Focus on living in the present.
4	Creative inspiration Desire/opportunity to achieve potential Fulfill the gap / hole with what is missing	Shame Rejection Boredom Feeling of a wasted/ meaningless / purposeless life	Interjection to avoid being ordinary and maintain image of uniqueness and authenticity. Emotional internalization of idealized work, experiences, or personal relationships to avoid feelings of deficiency. Self-blame for relationship failures, feeding feelings of unworthiness and inadequacy.	Stay focused in the moment and what is positive about it, especially when attention goes to the negative or to what is missing. Breathe and engage in artistic endeavors to ground self into body. Commit to productive, meaningful, good work.

Figure 12-1 | Cutler & Purcell Grief/Loss/Change Process by Enneagram Type

The How and Why: Taking Care of Business With The Enneagram

	MOVES TOWARDS	MOVES AWAY FROM	DEFENSE MECHANISM & BEHAVIORAL MANIFESTATION	DEVELOPMENT PRACTICE
5	More opportunity for time Better health	Paralysis Sense of feeling stuck or constrained	Isolation to promote image of being knowledgeable and avoid inner emptiness. Physical withdrawal from others and focus on acquiring knowledge while avoiding relationships and compartmentalizing feelings.	Get in touch with own emotions and body by engaging in a sport or creative activity. Ask for what is wanted. Practice living with "not knowing." Stand own ground and breathe when noticing the desire to withdraw.
6	Idealism/mission Long-term desire to achieve something	Problem/pain/danger Escape a bad situation	Projection to avoid rejection and maintain self-image of being loyal. Use of selective information to justify positive and/or negative feelings projected on others to assure safety and justify loyalty/fear/distrust.	When feeling doubt, reclaim it through faith in self and the world. Cultivate safety in self, without relying on others. Engage in regular physical activity and practice breathing to further ground self.
7	Freedom Openness to something else Fun	Confinement Restriction Crises no longer able to be rationalized or reframed as positive	Rationalization to avoid pain and suffering and maintain self-image of being OK. Positive reframes of negative experiences, focusing on an even better potential future.	Practice staying in the moment rather than moving into future planning.
8	Joy Something better Receiving something Self-care Surrender/relaxing/opening up	Intellectual boredom	Denial to avoid vulnerability and to support self-image of being strong. Focus on impacting others rather than being receptive to them.	Act with self-restraint and allow self to focus on own sadness and vulnerability. Engage in physical activity to productively release anger. Refer to a picture of self as a child to access feelings of vulnerability and sadness. Discuss with a trusted friend.
9	Shock Lists (Flexible) Deadlines Un-demanded love	Health crisis Family crisis	Narcotization to avoid conflict and maintain self-image of being harmonious and comfortable, leading to inertia, self-forgetting, and absence from relationships.	Practice being with, allowing, and acknowledging own feeling of loss. Acknowledge the anger present into own life. Practice directness and clarity of communication. Engage in regular physical activity to bring up repressed feelings and emotions.

(Cutler & Purcell, 2015)

Figure 12-1 | Cutler & Purcell Grief/Loss/Change Process by Enneagram Type (continued)

Janine Cutler and Andrea Purcell map out the individual Enneatype defense responses and needs in the grief/change process in Figure 12-1. It is beneficial for managers and employees to know about these individual needs within the larger context so that they can address change from multiple angles. For example, while the overall organizational change communications can be guided by answering the questions above, managers can then work with their direct reports on a one-on-one basis to help them proceed through the change, taking into account their individual needs, and coaching/supporting them in undertaking the development practices identified by Cutler and Purcell.

Remember how in Chapter 10 we discussed the importance of a client's readiness to change, when confronted with 360-degree feedback and data? Well, it turns out that peoples' openness to and readiness for change may be related to their Enneagram type! Dirk Cloete, of Integrative Enneagram Solutions, has conducted some really interesting research, correlating Enneagram type from the iEQ9 to the Big Five Factors Personality Theory, and discovered the following when looking specifically at the "Openness vs. Traditional" mindset: Enneatypes 4, 7, and 8 (and to a slightly lesser extent 3s and 5s) are more comfortable with and amenable to change, whereas Enneatypes 9s (and to a lesser extent 1s, 2s, and 6s – the compliant/dutiful Hornevian triad) are less so. This insight is valuable for managers who want to make sure that they are providing what their people need as they are going through inevitable organizational changes. For example, this could imply that even further care and attention must be provided to the Enneatype 1s, 2s, 6s, and 9s on the team, to lead, support and encourage them through the change successfully, ensuring their needs and concerns are addressed.

PRACTITIONER NOTE

Additional anecdotal evidence to this has been witnessed when organizational transformations drag on for a prolonged period of time. In these circumstances, it has been observed that Enneatype 2s tend to seek out more immediate stability and appreciation from other outlets and opportunities, foregoing waiting for the change to play out and seeing where the cards land. The assertive triad Enneatypes (3s, 7s, and 8s) also tend to create their own destinies, especially during these times. Enneatype 9s tend to stick around to see what happens when the dust finally settles.

On a related note, the COVID-19 pandemic provided a live laboratory to test the world's resilience during a global health crisis, requiring self-isolation, limited social contact, and severe changes to customary independence, rituals, and freedoms. People responded to this situation of extreme change and stress according to their Enneagram type predilections.

These reports from Enneagram enthusiasts on social media provide insights that leaders and managers can use to help support, motivate, and engage their team members during times of stress or change that result in social isolation. This may become even more relevant in the near future, as organizations realize that remote work is not only possible, but may even be preferable … and can generate far greater benefits and cost savings than on-campus working. These benefits can include greater access to talent without geographic limitations and relocation expenses, decreased traffic and pollution, decreased costs associated with reduced travel and less need for office facilities, reduced environmental impact, etc.

TYPE	WHAT THEY MISS	THEIR COPING ACTIONS
1	Family connections Meeting friends for regular connections	Existing bonds to pull through Feeling that things are pretty much the same; enjoy the working from home and want to continue it, making do/making it work less, conserving, adapting Looking to what they can do to make it a happier and healthier time Seeing this as a nice break from providing in-person help all the time
2	Connecting with friends Sleep/rest (due to caring for others)	Virtual Happy Hours Baking, shopping for others Self-care, focusing on self and own needs Trying to focus on the positive that will come of this Desire to help in the front lines
3	Action, getting things done	Focus on being, rather than doing Image Finding moments of silence, connection, and beauty in the new "ordinary"
4	Unique zen environment Not having to worry about others Not being able to easily access tools for creativity outlets (project, hobbies) In-person, meaningful, authentic connections Concern about how the world will look after this	Recreate a zen environment at home: Clean, tidy home, flowers Focus on present and thankfulness, gratitude for what is, versus what was lost and glorification of the past Creating a separate work space Cross-stitching, meditating Jewelry, Reading, Comfort eating
5	Routine Frustration around lack of appropriate global/local response to the pandemic	Creating new routine, but very few changes to adhere to social/physical distancing/SIP (which was already the norm for them) Embracing comfortable clothes (pajamas, no bra)
6	Real-life contact/conversation Structure Time alone from family	Dipping into stockpiles and activating emergency plans Maintaining routines Overeating to quell anxieties
7	Missing out on everything, including people Freedom/independence in own space and travel Some fear about safety of own job, in terms of providing for continued independence	"Minimum viable pain" (the minimum it takes to prevent the pain of comments/critiques of others) Casual clothes Adopting sobriety and routine into life, getting used to doing more with less, and having gratitude for what they have without yearning for more or something else
8	Action, control, not being able to do what I want to do Nothing (no vulnerability) Carnal knowledge, physical contact	Bra-less (control what they still can, do what they want in areas where they weren't able to before because of societal expectations, rules), self-pleasure
9	Nothing! Meeting up with friends	Napping, Netflix, Narcotization, Pajamas, no make-up Withdrawal to regain energy Dissociating

Figure 12-2 | The Enneatypes in Isolation

Note that some companies' norms of "cameras always on" – designed to create a greater sense of connection between videoconference attendees – may actually be intrusive, stressful, and exhausting to some Enneatypes. Remember, too, that the limitations imposed by Shelter-in-Place guidelines may be harder for some Enneatypes that value their freedom and independence (i.e., 7s and 8s) than others. We may also expect the Hornevian dutiful/complaint triad (Enneatypes 1, 2, and 6) to best adhere to new rules and regulations, as best they can, despite their relatively higher aversion to change. That said, each person's individual home and life situation will impact his/her responses and needs in these types of stressful situations. This will necessitate managers to work with their individual team members to understand their individual situations and environments, and address their needs accordingly.

PRACTITIONER NOTE

As I have been trying to integrate different best practices together to a common core, it makes sense to me to look at and respond to events as if they were changes. For example, when delivering customer service training, it makes sense to follow a model based on the grief/loss cycle and its appropriate, facilitating behaviors. We have already seen that human beings proceed through four different phases (Denial, Resistance, Exploration, and Acceptance) when encountering a loss that affects them personally. A person's journey through these phases can be facilitated and eased with proper support and encouragement. At the denial stage, people need more information. Respected and trusted authorities need to provide consistent and constant communication about what is happening or what is about to happen. Provide as many details as possible to reinforce the inevitability of the change event.

When leaders see that employees have progressed from denial to resistance, they need to be as empathetic as possible to the employee plight and the difficulties that this change event is going to create for them, personally and directly.

When leaders see that employees are ready to explore options, they need to engage the employees in brainstorming of opportunities that the change event might create for them. Which of these are they interested in pursuing? If the employees aren't coming up with options, the leaders can help steer them towards some of which they are aware or can help create for them.

Finally, when leaders see that employees have advanced to the final stage of acceptance, it's important to recognize and appreciate the employees for having gone through this difficult process.

Customer recovery models also fit nicely within the change management framework. If we reframe a customer service incident as a loss (there was a disconnect between what the customer expected and what really happened), we can proceed through the four stages above to assist the customer to resolution.

Information must be collected up-front using consulting skills and active listening to glean, not only the presenting issue, but the underlying interests and concerns of the customer. Once the customer service agent has a solid understanding of the customer's issues and underlying interests (this is where the Enneagram comes in handy), s/he can respond empathically to the customer to make him/her feel heard and understood. The next step is to engage the customer in a conversation about what can be done. What does the customer want? What options are available? Can a solution be co-created so that the customer feels committed to it and in control (which is what they lost when the unexpected event occurred), rather than feeling victimized by whatever solution is being inflicted on him/her? Finally, when the right solution is attained, agreed upon, and implemented, it's imperative for the customer to be appreciated for his/her loyalty to the company and for sticking with the company through this experience.

The parallels between the Kübler-Ross grief/loss framework and the customer recovery model are remarkable – and they work! To drive the point home even more, and to integrate yet another framework around accountability, consider the Oz Principle of personal accountability. This framework calls out the natural human tendency to go "below the line" and adopt a victim mentality in times of change and adversity. By encouraging and coaching "above the line" behaviors and reactions, employees maintain a more positive outlook and develop greater ownership and accountability when encountering change events. According to the model, whenever we encounter a change event, we have the power of choice to See it, Own it, Solve it, and Do it. When we see something, we should focus on what the issue is and how we can affect it. We will not always have full authority and scope over being able to solve the entire problem, but it is likely that we have the ability to solve a component of it. We can then take ownership of that smaller component and create a solution to implement. This, too, perfectly aligns with the change management and customer service/recovery frameworks.

NOTE: It may be easier for people to understand the ever-mutating change process by shattering their already-embedded notions propagated by Kurt Lewin since the 1940s. Unfortunately, we no longer live in a time or world with the luxury of allowing the "refreezing" of a new way, process, system, etc. following the unfreezing of its predecessor and the implementation of the change. Instead, we encounter a world of slushiness, where nothing has the chance to re-solidify before another change is necessary. In this new environment, it becomes even more necessary to latch onto small slivers of ice within the slush, exemplifying the only solid state known, usually in the form of the organization's ultimate vision, mission, and/or operating principles.

Application of the Enneagram within these models serves to enhance our effectiveness in being able to help employees and customers navigate the difficulties they are facing. Knowing an employee's or customer's Enneagram type can help a leader or customer service agent to focus on the real underlying issues, which are most important to that individual. Just like in negotiation strategies, it's not the presenting issue or position that we need to deal with, but, more importantly, the underlying interest/concern. And that insight is only derived through relationship- and trust-building.

Chapter 13

Accountability

Accountability is a big issue facing our society these days, and is a pervasive challenge in our organizations. We all have our fair share of customer service horror stories that we divulge at social gatherings. And we all hope that our own companies don't become the targets or subjects of these conversations. So we undertake many measures and initiatives in our efforts to try to create the ideal environment for employees to be engaged and take responsibility in the workplace. We create job descriptions that delineate the roles and responsibilities of each position. We write SMART (Specific, Measurable, Achievable yet Aggressive, Realistic and Results-oriented, and Time-bound) goals that operationally define the standards to which employees will be held and the metrics by which their performance will be assessed at the end of the year. (See Chapter 4 for a refresher on this).

Indoctrinating employees into the Oz Principle framework of personal accountability (discussed in Chapter 12) is an effective approach to influence their mindset in a positive way. Motivating employees in accordance to what's fundamentally important and inspirational to them (discussed in Chapters 2 and 3) is a critical long-term strategy, too. A complementary tool that supports and intends to perpetuate accountability in the workplace is the RACI Matrix. The RACI Matrix is a practical way to document each stakeholder's exact role and involvement in each step of a process or project. The roles are:

- Responsible – the (ideally) one person who actually performs the specific task
- Accountable – the person who is ultimately accountable for the success of the process/project
- Consulted – anyone whose advice and input must be sought out for this step in the process/project
- Informed – anyone who needs to receive an FYI that this step/action has occurred

And sometimes:

- Support – anyone who may provide assistance to a Responsible party in completing that step of the project/process
- Omitted – anyone who has not current role in this particular step of the process/project, but who may have had a past and/or has a future role (usually R, C, I, or S)

A couple important ground rules of RACI are that we can only have one "A" and, ideally, one "R" called out per task/activity step. If it looks like there may be more than one "R" for the task, select one to be the actual "R" and assign "S" for the other(s) to support the "R" in the task's achievement.

PROJECT / PROCESS NAME TASK | ACTIVITY | PROJECT STEP	DUE BY	NAME 1	NAME 2	NAME 3	NAME 4	NAME 5	NAME 6	NAME 7	NAME 8	NAME 9	NAME 10
1.											
2.											
3.											
4.											
5.											
6.											
7.											
8.											
9.											
10.											

KEY: Assign letter(s) to each Stakeholder for each Task/Activity/Project Step per the key below. **Only one person can be designated as "A" (and ideally, one as "R") per Task/Activity/Project Step.**
R= Responsible (does the task) | A= Accountable (for the overall project's success) | C= Consulted (provides input on the task) | I= Informed (receives an FYI at this point)
S=Support (supports "R" in completing this task/activity/step) | O = Omitted (not involved in this task/activity/step, but is involved in others)

Figure 13-1 | RACI/RASCIO Matrix

Furthermore, the RACI is most effective when actual names are placed in each of the Stakeholder positions, although there may be times when a higher-level RACI needs to be created. After the RACI matrix is completed, it is recommended standard practice to disseminate the document to all of the stakeholders called out within it. This is necessary in order to ensure that everyone is aware about what is required and expected of him/her at every step of the process or project. Furthermore, everyone is then cognizant of how his/her action (or inaction) affects and impacts future steps and the other stakeholders.

For ideas on how to make work even more personally-meaningful to employees of each Enneatype, please revisit Chapter 3 (Recruitment, Engagement, and Retention), Chapters 4 and 5 (emphasizing alignment to the company's mission, vision, and values as components of Strategic Planning), and Chapter 8 (on Influence). And something that is applicable to all Enneagram types is the importance of clarity around the expectations of their managers and their organizations, as well as the repercussions for not meeting them. The responsibility for accountability goes both ways: a manager can't expect employees to read his/her mind about what s/he and the business needs from them, and employees can't assume that they know what their manager and organization need from them. Both parties need to work together and talk to each other, making sure that they are in alignment and agreement with each other about those explicit expectations, the potential rewards for their achievement, and consequences for lack of action. When followed through on, only then can a true culture of accountability, trust, and fairness be created and sustained.

The How and Why: Taking Care of Business With The Enneagram

PRACTITIONER NOTE

A fun and interactive experience to bring the RACI to life is to create a mock role play of the process. This helps the stakeholders gain a better understanding of all the moving parts of the process, while seeing how their role contributes to the bigger picture and end goal. It also helps create greater empathy for the other stakeholders and their needs. Ideally, bring the entire team together to walk through the process. Assign each member a respective role, according to his/her responsibility (R) in the process. If multiple people hold that same role, ask for one volunteer from the group to represent that role, while the others serve as advisors and observers during the role play. Play out the entire process, step-by-step, explicitly calling out the hand-offs and interdependencies. This is a great way to tap into the adult learning need for kinesthetic experience, as opposed to just visual or auditory. After all, adults learn best experientially. Furthermore, consider videotaping this exercise. This can memorialize the event, signal its importance, serve as a future refresher course, and help train newcomers in the process. Plus, it's fun!

PROCEED WITH CAUTION

There will be times when Human Resources and Organization Development practitioners will be asked by managers to intervene in situations that have already been determined to require "team-building" or "coaching" as their solution. We must be very cautious to conduct our own root cause analysis in these situations, especially when they are presented with already-established prognoses. Although team-building interventions are pretty low-risk at causing any additional damage, they may be insufficient in resolving the actual, underlying issue. I am reminded of a situation where a manager wanted team-building to counteract her team's lack of initiative. Also, I recall countless times when managers have reached out to me to conduct 360-degree feedback surveys or start coaching engagements with their direct reports with whom they are experiencing performance problems. While team-building will definitely help team members and their managers better understand each other, their varying motivations and work style preferences, and build concrete norms and rules of engagement, managers still have work to do. Furthermore, 360-degree feedback surveys and coaching engagements are intended as professional development experiences for employees who are seen as having the potential for a positive trajectory within the organization, not for remediation. Remediation and performance coaching are best performed by the stumbling employee's manager him/herself. It is the professional duty of the Human Resources or Organization Development practitioners to stand their ground in these situations and drive accountability to the managers to perform these important tasks and roles. We can and should, of course, coach the managers in what to do, but we should not be doing that work for them. First, this is part of their responsibilities as managers. Second, we don't want to create or perpetuate the perception that when someone receives coaching from HR or OD, s/he is on his/her way out of the company. Too many times, frustrated managers turn and defer to HR or OD to fix a problem as a last resort.

They may even do this to create the image of having given the employee every opportunity to succeed, even engaging HR/OD. Whereas, in reality, they may already have given up on the employee. This can be taken as a great opportunity for HR and OD practitioners to drive accountability to the managers, supporting them in these coaching tasks, as necessary.

COACHING FOR ACCOUNTABILITY

As organizations struggle with the concept of accountability, one of the root causes that seems to contribute to this phenomenon is lack of employee clarity about what it is that they're actually being held accountable for. The constantly-changing VUCA environment in which we operate only exacerbates this challenge. To ensure that leaders and their teams are constantly aligned and can prioritize their work according to the latest developments and needs, leaders and managers can consider asking these coaching questions at every one-on-one check-in meeting:

- What is your understanding of our team's current priorities and what is expected of you in your role to achieve them?
- What are you currently working on to support these?
- What are you working on that does not support these?

- What will you stop doing to refocus on this quarter's priorities?
- What will you start or continue doing to meet the goals of this quarter's priorities?
- What support do you need to make this happen?
- How can we make sure that we hold each other accountable to these commitments? What happens if/when we don't?

These coaching questions don't take long to ask and answer. Regular check-ins (weekly or biweekly) where these questions are reviewed and updated can make a huge impact in ensuring clarity and alignment around expectations, and effecting course-corrections sooner rather than later, when it may be too late. This process drives accountability by increasing clarity, trust among colleagues (as everyone aligns to the same ultimate goals), and reducing frustrations and unnecessary swirl.

PRACTITIONER NOTE

When accountability is the presenting issue, it's usually coupled with its bff, trust. In order to ultimately get to accountability, the underlying issue of trust must be addressed first.

Once one of my client groups became ready to tackle their trust and accountability issues, I created the space and opportunity for them to address this elephant in the room. To validate my theory that these senior leadership team (SLT) members were unclear about expectations of them by their

The How and Why: Taking Care of Business With The Enneagram

leader and organization, didn't fully trust each other, and didn't believe that their colleagues were accountable, I conducted anonymous Zoom polls, asking:

- "I trust my LT colleagues implicitly." (Always, Sometimes. Never)
- "I trust my fellow LT colleagues to come through with what's expected of them." (Always, Sometimes, Never)
- "I am very clear about what my functional clients expect of me and my team." (Yes, Somewhat, No)
- "I am very clear about what our CXO expects of me and my team." (Yes, Somewhat, No)

Not suprisingly, the poll results showed that, for each question, roughly half of the SLT members reported needing more clarity around expectations, didn't fully trust their colleagues, and did not believe them to be accountable. We now had a clear burning platform.

Next, I introduced them to the Enneagram. Knowing each individual team member's Enneagram type allowed me to break the SLT into three fairly evenly-numbered groups according to their centers - one for the heart/feeling center (Enneatypes 2, 3, and 4), one for the head/thinking center (Enneatypes 5, 6, and 7), and one for the body/action center (Enneatypes 8, 9, and 1). Note that it will be very rare to have representation of all Enneatypes on all teams; we were, indeed, missing four of them. The groups reviewed Ralph Colby's Elements of Trust™ (1973) model, decided on their own individual scores of each element that they valued most in others in determining their trustworthiness, and reported out an average score for their group for each element. The full team debrief yielded the fascinating realization that trust meant different things to different people, and that those differences could be attributed to their Enneagram centers:

- The heart/feeling types (in this case, 2s and 3s) placed more emphasis on relational, respect, and recognition factors related to Acceptance:

others' empathy, listening, mistake tolerance, and non-judgment. They ranked Congruence factors lowest.
- The head/thinking types (in this case, 7s) placed a lot more focus on Congruence factors - around others' honesty and ethics, sincerity, clear rules and boundaries, and "walking the talk." They ranked the Acceptance factors lowest.
- The body/action types (in this case, 8s and 9s) were far more interested in Reliability factors - others taking agreed-to action, keeping promises/commitments, meeting deadlines, and being on time. They ranked the Openness factors - others' receptivity to others' ideas/opinions and willingness to disclose what's on their minds - lowest.

Using the team's new understanding of the diversity of how their colleagues perceived and built trust, they co-created team norms and agreements to guide and remind themselves about expectations of how to act in order to become a more fully trusting, trusted, and accountable senior leadership team.

Chapter 14

Conflict Management

Conflict can be defined as a disagreement between two or more people resulting in a negative emotion. According to Tricia Jones and Ross Brinkert's Comprehensive Conflict Coaching Model, there are three basic factors that contribute to conflict:
- Self/Identity/Role
- Trigger/Motivation/Reaction
- Actionability

The resolution relies upon our being able to step outside of our skin and take on another person's perspective. Recall the Platinum Rule discussed in Chapter 2? The Enneagram can, obviously, help provide us with insight in this arena.
- How do I see myself/my role/my purpose?
- How does s/he see me/my role/my purpose?
- What behaviors are triggering my reaction?
- Which of my behaviors is/are triggering him/her?
- Who has the power to fix this situation or make it better?
- What is within the scope of my control to do to fix this situation or make it better?

Managing conflict productively entails:
- Identifying Potential Conflicts and their Causes
- Controlling our Emotions to prevent escalation
- Responding Appropriately
- Compete (assertive, uncooperative)
- Collaborate (assertive, cooperative)
- Compromise (intermediate assertiveness and cooperation)
- Accommodate (unassertive, cooperative)
- Avoid (unassertive, uncooperative)
- Taking Action
- Mediating, as Needed
- Managing the Solution and Moving Forward

Knowledge of the Enneagram can help us in identifying the probable default preferred response style for each of the Enneatypes. For example, the Hornevian Triad of Assertive/Aggressive/Expansive includes Enneatypes 3, 7, and 8. Superimposing them over the Thomas-Kilmann Conflict Mode Instrument (TKI), we would expect to experience these three Enneatypes in either the "Competing" or "Collaborating" sectors, high on the Thomas-Kilmann "Assertiveness" axis. Level of cooperation may then come into play in predicting toward which sector each of these Enneatypes would gravitate. Seeing conflict as a stressor for all Enneatypes (but probably not as much for Enneatype 8s), we could also include the Enneatypes who align with Enneatypes 3, 7, and 8 under stress in these areas. Therefore, we may also

The How and Why: Taking Care of Business With The Enneagram

see Enneatypes 6, 5, and 2 in these areas, especially under stress. Karen Horney categorizes Enneatypes 1, 2, and 6 as the Compliant/Idealistic/Abiding/Dutiful Triad. This would equate to being placed high on the Thomas-Kilmann "Cooperativeness" axis, encompassing the "Collaborating" and "Accommodating" conflict styles. Karen Horney classifies Enneatypes 4, 5, and 9 as the Withdrawn/Detached/Resigned Triad. This triad might be at home in the low "Assertiveness" and low "Cooperative" quadrant of "Avoiding" in the Thomas-Kilmann framework. This is where we might also find Enneatypes 1, 8, and 3 in stress. Many factors and individual differences amongst people will impact in which of these five areas they will likely land in any given situation. However, this should provide a decent start in our strategy of how to best approach a potentially contentious situation with someone with whose Enneagram type and motivations we are already familiar.

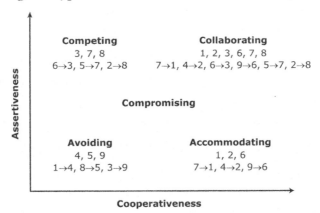

Figure 14-1 | Thomas-Kilmann Conflict Mode Instrument (TKI) and Enneagram Correlates

While the Hornevian Triads seem applicable to the Thomas-Kilmann model, the Harmonic Triads also come into play in conflict management. Judith O'Connor and Bruce Anderson also observe the alignment of the Enneagram with the Thomas-Kilmann Conflict Mode model. However, they interpret and present a model that differs slightly from the one I have depicted above. They concur that Enneatypes 4, 5, and 9 favor the "Avoiding" or "Withdrawing" area, but instead see Enneatypes 1, 3, and 8 at the "Competing" point. They place Enneatypes 2, 6, and 7 at the "Accommodating" point. They, too, warn against getting stuck in approaching conflict from only one modality, and instead selecting and using the one appropriate to the situation at hand.

Spencer Chernick (2016) also took on the challenge of correlating Enneagram types to TKI styles and came up with the following three statistically-significant findings in his study:

- Enneatypes 2 and 9 were more likely to adopt the Accommodating TKI style; Enneatypes 4 and 8 were least likely to adopt this conflict mode.
- Enneatype 9s were also more likely to adopt the Avoiding TKI style; Enneatype 8s were least likely to do so.
- Enneatype 8s were more likely to adopt the Competing TKI style; Enneatypes 2 and 9 were least likely to adopt this style.
- Chernick found no statistically-significant relationships for any Enneagram type in his sample toward the Collaborative and Compromising TKI styles.

The How and Why: Taking Care of Business With The Enneagram

Incorporating all of these insights, the Collaborating style of Enneatypes 1, 2, 3, 6, 7, and 8 – or Enneatypes 7, 4, 6, 9, 5, and 2 under stress – may be appropriate in situations where all parties are open to explore their concerns and when we want to build committed and cooperative relationships.

Enneatypes 3, 7, and 8 – or Enneatypes 6, 5, and 2 under stress – can use the Competing style most effectively in emergency or crisis situations, where immediate action is necessary and there may be no time for input and negotiation. It is also a viable option when it becomes apparent that the other party is taking advantage of our cooperative behavior.

The Compromising style is recommended when both parties have equal power and their goals don't align, in times when a deadline is approaching fast and a practical solution is needed. Adopting this style can have us show up as rational and reasonable, and can help us learn something from a difficult situation. This could be a viable option for Enneatype 5s or 8s under stress.

The Accommodating style is ideal in situations where the maintenance of harmony and stability are required. This seems like a go-to strategy for the dutiful Enneatypes 1, 2, and 6 – and Enneatypes 7, 4, and 2 under stress.

When the conflict involves trivial matters or when it seems best to let flaring tempers cool down, the Avoiding mode, associated with Enneatypes 4, 5, and 9 – or Enneatypes 1, 8, and 3 under stress – may serve as the right course of inaction.

Whatever a person's, or a team's, Enneatype affiliation tends to be, a recommended flow for progressing through

any conflict is to look at the Harmonic triads and channel or tap into:
- The Reactive triad's Enneatype 4, 6, and 8 energy to address the emotions and feelings that are triggered or brought up in the conflict, ensuring all voices are heard, and clarifying the issue at stake
- The Positive Outlook triad's Enneatype 2, 7, and 9 energy to explore all opportunities and possibilities, overcoming any negativity resulting from the conflict
- The Competency triad's Enneatype 1, 3, and 5 energy to select and implement a rational and logical solution.

Following this flow, teams can cool-headedly resolve conflicts, having healthily listened to everyone's concerns and considered a variety of options.

To help frame the situation and identify which modality to use, Curt Micka shows that difficult conversations involved in conflict management and peacemaking are comprised of three concurrent internal conversations:
- What happened? Who is responsible? This evokes the Competency Harmonic Triad of Enneatypes 1, 3, and 5.
- How do I feel about this? What emotions is this causing in me? This is related to the Intensity/Reactivity Harmonic Triad of Enneatypes 4, 6, and 8.
- How does this affect my identity? How does this affect my feelings of being a competent person? This applies to all Enneatypes.

The How and Why: Taking Care of Business With The Enneagram

Note, too, the close affiliation to the Comprehensive Conflict Coaching Model laid out above.

Enneatype-based insight into each Enneatype's conflict transformation "baggage" has been summarized by Louise Phipps Senft, Esq.:

- Enneatype 1 Rigidity: "Why are you choosing that? It's not the right thing to do."
- Enneatype 2 Manipulation: "How can you not be friends after all of this hard work?"
- Enneatype 3 Impatience: "So, are you ready to decide and move on yet?"
- Enneatype 4 Insufficiency: "So, how does this make you feel? That is so ordinary and superficial – there must be something else deeper and more meaningful here ..."
- Enneatype 5 Labored Thinking: "You're moving too fast. You should have all the data before you do anything, and you should take more time to think through things before taking action."
- Enneatype 6 Suspicion: "But, are you absolutely certain you want to do that? What if ..."
- Enneatype 7 Avoidance of Pain: "Are you sure you want to make decisions rather than continue to explore all the exciting possibilities? Let's try ..."
- Enneatype 8 Direction ("My way!"): "Let me tell you ... And that is just the way it is and how it's going to be."
- Enneatype 9 Distraction: "Did you say something? I think I just spaced out for a minute ... Don't push me around."

Taking these insights into consideration prior to engaging in a situation of potential conflict can help us prepare for what to expect and how to respond in order to get the best possible outcome. Furthermore, applying our understanding of the Enneagram, as it pertains to what each Enneatype is likely to fundamentally want and how each Enneatype is likely to react, can help us frame our interactions and discourse along these issues, rather than falling into the position-based trap. Negotiating around the actual underlying issues instead of our and our opponent's positions on them is far more effective and productive.

Managing Our Own Internal Reactions to Conflict

So what happens when we want to suppress our own frustrations (which may spill over to creating conflict with others)? This may be especially applicable to the "Anger" types, Enneatypes 8, 9, and 1.

Albert Ellis proposes a system that comes into play when we recognize ourselves getting triggered by a dissonance between what we think *should, ought to,* or *must* be happening versus what is actually occurring. (Recall the Enneatype 1's fondness for using the word "should" and their annoyance over things that don't comply with what *should be*). This highlights Ellis's premise that we get frustrated over our own irrational beliefs and expectations about events rather than the actual events themselves. Instead, Ellis recommends following his ABCDE technique whereby we:

- Recognize the Adversity when we encounter the Activating Event.

- Identify the irrational Belief around the adversity, which we believe shouldn't be happening to us (although there was never a promise or guarantee of this!).
- Realize the Consequences emanating from our irrational beliefs (usually frustration or anger).
- Dispute the irrational belief by reminding ourselves that the universe never promised us a life devoid of frustrations, hassles, and troubles. We survived up to this point and we will continue to survive.
- Reap the positive benefits of the Effects of changing our beliefs and behaviors.

By consciously altering our beliefs, we can change the consequences that align to them. Enneatypes 8, 9, and 1 don't maintain a monopoly on being easily frustrated, annoyed, or disappointed; we can all learn to grow using Ellis's ABCDE technique.

Curt Micka also presents a four-part self-administered questionnaire to optimize our chances for a successful outcome in conflict management experiences:

1. What is my part in the conflict?
2. How do I feel about what is going on?
3. What can I do to change this dynamic?
4. How can I maintain my presence during this conflict?

These questions are very evocative of the accountability models discussed earlier (recall the Oz Principle in Chapter 12). These topics are all very much inter-related, no?

R. Karl Hebenstreit, Ph. D.

PRACTITIONER NOTE

In *Crucial Conversations: Tools for Talking When Stakes Are High*, Kerry Patterson, Joseph Grenny, Ron McMillan, and Al Switzler present several frameworks to optimize mutual understanding and successful outcomes in potentially-volatile situations. One great take-away that can be applied to productive and proactive conflict management, as well as during coaching and feedback, involves stating up-front what we don't want the recipient of our feedback to think or feel. This, obviously, is dependent on our ability to empathize with our partner. Knowledge of the Enneagram will help in these difficult situations since we may have advanced insight into what may trigger or bring up fear in our partner. Taking care to avoid triggering those defenses, by calling out that our intent is not to do so, shows that we understand and care about the other person. We are explicitly indicating that we are not there to cause or inflict intentional pain, but, instead, to provide productive feedback or advice for the other's development and future success.

Chapter 15

The Process Enneagram and Organization Design

Human Resources and Organization Development practitioners and organization leaders will, at many points in their careers, be involved in reviewing the efficacy of their departments, organizations, and processes in order to recommend changes to improve or enhance them. Richard Knowles's interpretation of the Enneagram framework through a process lens can be very helpful in this charge. The Process Enneagram can be applied to assess the organization in terms of:

- Identity (Enneagram Points 0 and 9)
- Intentions (Enneagram Point 1)
- Tension Issues (Enneagram Point 2)
- Relationships and Connections (Enneagram Point 3)
- Principles and Standards (Enneagram Point 4)
- The Work Itself (Enneagram Point 5)
- Information (Enneagram Point 6)
- Learning (Enneagram Point 7)
- New Context, Structures, and Strategies (Enneagram Point 8)

Knowles separates the Enneagram's inner triangle (point 3, 6, and 9) as factors that impact everything people do in any living system. Recall how these play out in resolving conflict (see Chapter 14). The other Enneagram points are employed as follows:

Lack of clarity around identity (9) and intentions, or mission (1), lead to people getting stuck in issues (2). The Process Enneagram uses an internal triangle, comprised of Enneapoints 2, 8, and 5, to describe organizational "command and control" systems. To get unstuck, we move from Enneapoint 2 to Enneapoint 8 to try to resolve the issues by dictating a solution and structure. Our solution is imposed between Enneapoints 8 and 5. This creates further conflict between Enneapoints 5 and 2, as people argue about how and why to do the work. The conflict is inherently between the organization's command and control style and peoples' innate tendency to self-organize.

The solution, therefore, is an outcome of this formula:
- Communication to develop clarity around our mission of who we are and what we're here to do (Enneapoint 1)
- Establishment and agreement to norms and rules of engagement (Enneapoint 4)
- Discussion of the issues based on our identity, mission, and rules of engagement (Enneapoint 2)
- Self-organization (including group organization), according to the context of the work (Enneapoint 8)
- Performance of the work (Enneapoint 5)
- Development of better ways of getting the work done (Enneapoint 7)
- Integration of experiences and knowledge into our evolving identity and continued growth

The How and Why: Taking Care of Business With The Enneagram

This interpretation and application of the Enneagram framework is useful in addressing a variety of organizational challenges. The Process Enneagram can be used to support team development work (see Chapter 11), helping to clarify roles, objectives, the team mission, norms, and the work to be done. It can also be applied to productive conflict resolution (see Chapter 14), in assessing the health and effectiveness of an organization and its processes (see Chapter 11's 9 Domains Framework), in strategic planning considerations (see Chapter 4), and even when driving accountability through the development and evaluation of process flows and RACI matrices (see Chapters 12 and 13). Furthermore, it has implications for use in organization design, especially when considering the ineffectiveness of the command and control style in relation to the human need to self-organize.

Galbraith's Star Model is arguably the seminal go-to for organization design work. And yet this model and process, too, can be enhanced with insights gleaned from the Enneagram. To start, the foundational work around the organization's values (see Chapter 5) can be used to develop the desired design criteria for the new organization structure. Once the criteria are known, the strategic planning work (see Chapter 4) can be referenced to bring forward the strategy, from which the rest of the organization design process flows.

It all begins with Strategy, equivalent to Knowles's Enneapoints 9 and 1. Identity comprises Knowles's interpretation of Enneapoint 9, with its subsequent movement

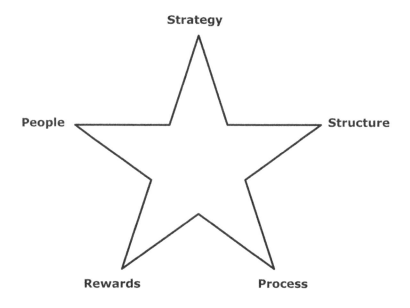

Figure 15-1 | Galbraith's (1977) Star Model

to Intentionality at Enneapoint 1, setting in motion the 1-4-7 triangle. Enneapoints 1, 4, and 7, are all about strategy and capabilities, respectively espousing directionality of the organization, the unique niche it fills, and its vision. The second point of the star relates to Structure, which ultimately deals with power (Enneapoint 8), as part of the 2-5-8 triangle. The third point of the star deals with the Processes and information (Enneapoint 5) that need to be put in place to fill the gaps that the structure doesn't adequately address. The third point of the star deals with Rewards and reward systems (Enneapoints 2 and 3, marking the overlap with and beginning of the 3-6-9 triangle) that will help motivate People, including Human Resources policies (the rules pertaining to the tribe at Enneapoint 6), the last point of the star. And that leads us back to ... Enneapoint 9, Strategy.

Chapter 16

The Enneagram in Agility

The constantly-escalating Volatility, Uncertainty, Complexity, and Ambiguity (VUCA) of the global environment has led companies to flock to find a solution in agility. (Note that agility is differentiated from Agile methodology in that the former is a mindset of being, whereas the latter is an action of doing – specifically a process originated in software development and project management). It is fascinating to see that the Enneagram can provide a map to the concepts touted in the agility mindset, in which companies are investing their futures. When working with an organization that has embraced the Enneagram, it is easy to show them how the system can also help them develop a more agile mindset through the adoption of these principles, all related to the virtues of each Enneatype:

1. One of the key tenets of agility is the importance of finding some element of stability to latch on to, in a world that is otherwise spiraling in chaos. This stability usually shows up in the form of a True North, meaning an overarching, inspirational vision or mission, bolstered by operating/decision principles to help in prioritization of competing goals – all associated with Enneapoint

1. Another key learning from Enneapoint 1 is that perfection is the enemy of progress. In the world of agility, the goal is for good enough, instead of perfect. The Pareto Principle, where 80% is good enough (since it takes 20% of energy and effort to attain that point, and an additional 80% to attempt to achieve that final, elusive 20%) is a relevant takeaway from Enneapoint 1, especially when it leads to the development of a Minimum Viable Product (MVP).
2. One of the gifts and superpowers of Enneapoint 2 is the ability to intuitively know and meet others' needs. Focusing on customers' needs is another tenet of agility. So much so, that they are included every step of the way, especially during sprints to brainstorm and develop new ways of working to meet their needs. Validating what we think our customers and stakeholders need and value from us is critical in determining the best path forward. That requires their involvement and input in every step along the way, not just at the end or later on down the road, where, based on bad or untested assumptions, we may have veered off in the wrong direction and totally missed the mark.
3. Enneapoint 3 is all about achieving goals in the most expedient and efficacious ways. The elements of time-boxing (allocating specific, short amounts of focused time for specific tasks), focusing on outcomes, fit-for-purpose meetings and outputs, and speed all fall into the sweet spot of this domain. Focus on efficiency

also serves to drive stopping low-value activities and to simplifying solutions. Speed is another tenet of agility, and we must remember that sometimes we need to slow down in order to make sure we are going in the right direction (for which we need to tap into the energies of Enneapoints 4 and 9).

4. Agility is all about coming up with new and better ways of thinking and working, often by eliminating noise and focusing on the important core. This concept of authentic creativity is the essence of Enneapoint 4. This creativity is achieved through the activation of small, diverse teams of specialists, also components of Enneatype 4, coming together in sprints to create solutions. These activities can also serve to check forward movement that may be too fast, so that the teams can be assured that they are proceeding in the appropriate direction.

5. Enneapoint 5 teaches us about the importance of learning. In terms of agility, this takes place through retrospectives and in knowing and being curious about the business. Routine and ritual are also key components of agility, both important aspects of Enneatype 5 DNA. Agility also calls for experimentation in 90 day increments, then applying the learnings to determine future action, continuation in the same direction or change of course.

6. Trust is a foundational factor for any relationship, and the workplace isn't exempt from that requirement.

Enneapoint 6 reminds us that the price of admission for agility is trust in our colleagues and partners, and that we must always assume their good intentions. One of the lessons Enneatype 6s need to learn is tolerance for ambiguity through trust. VUCA literally has ambiguity within it. One of the signature back-up/contingency plans for Enneatype 6s, when faced with a failure or learning, is to pivot to another strategy or tactic, and to tap into the Enneapoint 7 energy to help them do so.

7. In addition to being natural visionaries, Enneatype 7s thrive in change and are known to be able to pivot on a dime. Therefore, the qualities of adaptability and flexibility, both major tenets of agility, reside at Enneapoint 7.

8. A mindset of agility requires boldness, and there is no Enneatype as bold as 8s. Boldness in experimentation and risk-taking is essential to ultimate innovation. Another lesson that Enneapoint 8 teaches us is that we should focus on what we can control and what is in our domain/sphere of influence. Success also necessitates building empowered teams and networks that have the autonomy and freedom to deliver results, all of these related to Enneapoints 7 and 8.

9. Iteration and routine rituals are key concepts in agility. And nobody does iteration and routine better than Enneatype 9. Taking the inputs and considerations proffered by their stakeholders at Enneapoint 2, we can invoke the strength of Enneapoint 9 in integrating

those recommendations in the next version of the work product/MVP. This, of course, also has connection to the concept of continuous improvement related to Enneapoint 9's neighbor, Enneapoint 1. Enneatype 1s find comfort in routine rituals, which help achieve balance and harmony by bringing people together to collaborate and align on what to focus on next.

The agility mindset is clearly very much aligned to the teachings of the Enneagram. In a world of continuous change and the constant introduction of new Organization Development models, having a way to relate new principles to an existing familiar and tried-and-true framework may offer our overwhelmed clients a glimmer of hope, comfort, relief, and greater understanding.

PRACTITIONER NOTE

The increased focus on agile ways of working relies on continuous and honest feedback – an extension of Enneapoint 5 above. Traditional agile practices for providing feedback follow the formula of "What I like about your proposal is ... Have you considered ...?" This process works well during sprints and in ensuring the "what" or output, but may not be the best for day-to-day team member interactions, which impact "how" the work is getting done between team members. Factoring in an environment that prevents employees from providing honest and direct feedback (due to relationship-oriented, people-pleasing or fear-based cultures) creates added complexity in achieving the ultimate benefits of going agile. I've found that bringing members of pods, squads, and work product teams together to address these important logistics and create agreements early

The How and Why: Taking Care of Business With The Enneagram

and head-on helps to set them up for success. Consider empowering the team members to review existing, traditional feedback methodologies (i.e., SBI, sandwich model, etc.) in relation to how the organization's culture helps and/or impedes their use and effectiveness. Then, factor in individual team member preferences for feedback based on their Enneagram types. The team can then contract explicitly as to how they will provide and receive feedback from each other, including how often and at what critical points in time (like end of project, daily, quarterly, etc.).

Epilogue

The concepts and frameworks presented in the preceding pages are a collection and sampling of some current and seminal best practices in the fields of Organization Development. They were amassed during my 25+ year career in Human Resources and Organization Development, having worked in and with a variety of large global companies, spanning multiple industries. Most of these models were used in most of these companies. It is by no means meant to be a comprehensive or exhaustive list. I have attempted to show that each of these frameworks can become more robust, meaningful, and effective by layering in insights and learning from the Enneagram. These insights include some that I have developed during my experiences of studying and applying the Enneagram in organizations, as well as the great work of many innovative Enneagram practitioners around the world (check out the "References and Additional Resources" section for further reading). It is my sincere hope that this compilation will inspire managers, Human Resources and Organization Development practitioners, and students of Industrial/Organizational Psychology and Organization

The How and Why: Taking Care of Business With The Enneagram

Development to integrate these insights and methodologies in the advancement and betterment of their own organizations and practices. And that they further grow, hone, and share their own experiences and enhancements to contribute to our continuous learning and understanding of this very complex and deep system, while reaping the benefits of its powerful insights to drive more effective, efficient, and sustainable business results and relationships.

R. Karl Hebenstreit, Ph. D.

Appendix A | You Know You're Accessing Enneagram Type ... If/When ...

ENNEATYPE	IF/WHEN...
1 Perfectionist / Reformer	You hear a loud "Internal Critic" voice inside your head that's always pointing out what's wrong and what needs to be fixed or improved (which contributes to your ability to easily and naturally discern differences between things). The worst thing someone can do to you is have you work for an immoral/unethical leader/company or ask you to go against your values.
2 Helper / Giver	You intuitively know what other people need and provide it to them, putting their needs before yours. The worst thing someone can do to you is make you feel irrelevant/unneeded/replaceable, or that your assistance and contributions are unappreciated or undervalued. You have left relationships (work or personal) because you were made to feel that way.
3 Performer / Achiever	You are very goal-oriented and will do whatever it takes to meet it, morphing to fit the situation's requirements. The worst thing that someone can do to you is prevent you from reaching your goal and/or harm your image/reputation/brand.
4 Artist / Romantic	You feel everyone else's emotions and feelings very deeply and uniquely as if they were your own, especially melancholy. The worst thing that someone can do to you is treat you as if you are common, not unique, or not special.
5 Observer / Analyst	You are really good at collecting and analyzing data to make it make sense. You have an internal circuit breaker switch that can be tripped at any time (even mid-sentence) if you're overly stimulated, causing you to need to exit the situation immediately to recharge your internal battery. The worst thing that someone can do to you is change your environment and/or surprise you with public spotlight/recognition.
6 Loyal Skeptic	You identify all possible threats, sources of danger, and things that could go wrong in any/every situation, and come up with contingency plans should that worst-case scenario materialize. This contributes to your excellent planning ability. The worst thing that someone can do is cause a break in your trust in them and/or threaten your comfort/security (i.e., job loss, injury).
7 Enthusiast / Epicure / Adventurer	You are really great at looking at the bright side of every situation, seeing and taking advantage of opportunities/possibilities, coming up with visionary ideas, and getting others excited to follow you. You put off making decisions because you see it as a constraining limit and want to keep all of your options open until the last minute to make sure you're not missing out on the best/most fun opportunity. The worst thing that someone can do to you is impose limits on you, your freedom, and/or your work.
8 Boss / Challenger / Protector	You excel at leading and executing plans through others. You actively seek out and engage in debate, conflict, and difficult situations as a natural part of life that must be dealt with and overcome/plowed through. Power, control, authority, and justice are of paramount importance to you. The worst thing that someone can do is take away your power/control, mistreat/hurt members of your inner circle, or impact your "turf."
9 Mediator / Peacekeeper	You have difficulty making decisions and/or taking a position because you see the benefit of, and good in, all choices and the whole system. The worst thing that someone can do to you is affect your status quo with major disruptive conflict and change.

Appendix B | Enneagram Types, Subtypes, Counter-Types, and Look-Alikes

TYPE	SELF-PRESERVATION	SOCIAL	1:1
1	Self-critical worrier	5ish *Unadapting role model*	8ish *Zealous reformer of others*
2	4ish/6ish *Not as concerned about connection*	3ish/8ish Knowledge, Competence, Influence	1:1/Sexual/Transmitting 4
3	1ish/6ish Efficient, Autonomous, Workaholic, *Vain about not being vain*	Socially polished and brilliant	2ish/7ish/8ish Charisma
4	1ish/3ish/5ish/7ish *Stoicism around suffering, Happiest 4s*	Sad 4, 6ish Most suffering, feeling, emotional	7ish/8ish Makes others suffer, Competitive
5	Warmest 5 Minimalist	7ish High ideals Need for shared knowledge	4ish *Most romantic, emotional, intense, artistic Highest need to connect*
6	2ish/9ish Most phobic	1ish/3ish Obedient, seek protection, authority	8ish Fight/aggressive *Counter-phobic*
7	6ish *Network of allies, Materialistic, Cheerful, Talkative*	2ish/8ish/Social 9ish *Anti-gluttony through service to others*	9ish/5ish Search for ideal experiences
8	5ish Down-to-earth	2ish women, 8ish men More mellow, sociable	Center of attention *Most emotional*
9	8ish Satisfy physical needs	2ish/3ish Support the group	4ish Fuses with others Most emotional 9

Countertypes in italics.

Based on the work of Beatrice Chestnut, European Enneagram Conference, Copenhagen, Denmark, September 2015

R. Karl Hebenstreit, Ph. D.

Appendix C | The Enneagram with MBTI, DiSC, and Body Center Correlates

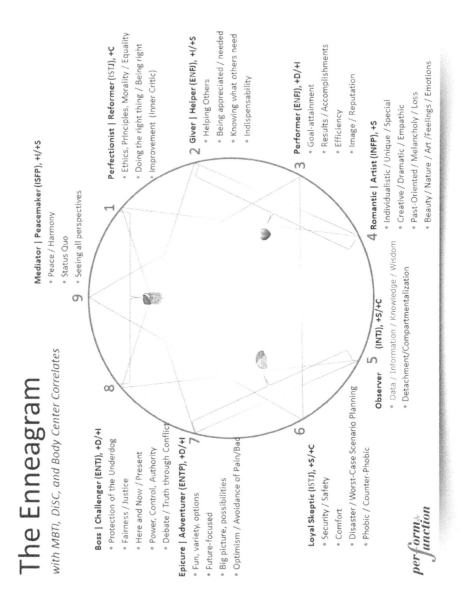

The Enneagram
with MBTI, DiSC, and Body Center Correlates

Mediator | Peacemaker (ISFP), +I/+S
- Peace / Harmony
- Status Quo
- Seeing all perspectives

Perfectionist | Reformer (ISTJ), +C
- Ethics, Principles, Morality / Equality
- Doing the right thing / Being right
- Improvement (Inner Critic)

Giver | Helper (ENFJ), +I/+S
- Helping Others
- Being appreciated / needed
- Knowing what others need
- Indispensability

Performer (ENFJ), +D/+I
- Goal-attainment
- Results / Accomplishments
- Efficiency
- Image / Reputation

Romantic | Artist (INFP), +S
- Individualistic / Unique / Special
- Creative / Dramatic / Empathic
- Past-Oriented / Melancholy / Loss
- Beauty / Nature / Art /Feelings / Emotions

Observer (INTJ), +S/+C
- Data / Information / Knowledge / Wisdom
- Detachment/Compartmentalization

Loyal Skeptic (ISTJ), +S/+C
- Security / Safety
- Comfort
- Disaster / Worst-Case Scenario Planning
- Phobic / Counter-Phobic

Epicure | Adventurer (ENTP), +D/+I
- Fun, variety, options
- Future-focused
- Big picture, possibilities
- Optimism / Avoidance of Pain/Bad

Boss | Challenger (ENTJ), +D/+I
- Protection of the Underdog
- Fairness / Justice
- Here and Now / Present
- Power, Control, Authority
- Debate / Truth through Conflict

perform & function

Appendix D | Behavioral Interview Questions to Assess Emotional Intelligence

TYPE	QUESTION: Tell me a recent time when you... What did you do? What was the outcome? What could have been done differently	Look For:
1	Were faced with an ethical dilemma. Were told by a superior to do something that you thought was wrong. Had to make a decision between right and wrong. Worked with someone who only thought in black/white, right/wrong terms.	• Understanding that there is not always a right/wrong answer and that there is a middle "grey" ground. • Solutions about finding what others value and showing how options relate to that • Ability to admit own mistakes and forgiving others for theirs.
2	Found yourself unable to say no to a peer or superior. Worked with someone who wouldn't say no to additional work requests and/or responsibilities.	• Understanding that a person's value is not dependent on what others think of them and the ability to push back and set limits appropriately.
3	Set a target/goal for yourself to achieve related to a better job, promotion/increase, new title, etc. How did you accomplish it? Worked with someone who was so driven to accomplish a goal that s/he cut some corners to make it happen.	• Evidence of collaborative and inclusive methodology in achieving goals, with appropriate credit to others who contributed to the success. • Identity not based on successes or accomplishments. • Humility.
4	Handled work relationships with highly-talented, creative coworkers who were also "high maintenance." Had to work with coworkers who dwell on how things used to be / be done in the past rather than how they are being done now.	• Ability to appreciate uniqueness and creativity while minimizing/managing drama. • Ability to refocus others on positive, present-based thinking rather than on how things were better in the past.
5	Were overwhelmed with leadership requests for data and metrics, so much so that it interfered with your ability to focus on the delivery of services to your customers.	• Ability to influence and persuade leader to identify and focus on what's important, express feelings, and take action rather than staying stuck in analysis paralysis.
6	Were confronted/presented with doubts and arguments about the success or effectiveness of one of your proposals. How did you counter the arguments and persuade the nay-sayers to proceed?	• Ability to identify and address root of challenger's concerns and obtain buy-in. • Ability to persuade others to move forward in a positive direction in spite of latent uncertainty / insecurity.
7	Worked with someone who was excellent at coming up with ideas and possibilities, yet never followed through with them? Worked with someone who was too immersed in him/herself and his/her own world rather than others'.	• Ability to harness vision into present-based thinking (including negatives) while creating accountability and clear next steps. • Ability to help others refocus and take others' opinions, perspectives, and experiences into account.
8	Worked with someone who bullied their peers into doing things their way? Worked with someone who micromanaged and insisted that everything go through him/her first?	• Ability to challenge / push back appropriately and not take others' challenges personally. • Ability to seek out and create win-win situations as well as facilitate compromise.
9	Worked with someone who had difficulty making decisions or reversed decisions on a regular basis?	• Flexibility and patience in working in an ambiguous, changing environment. • Ability to redirect and focus others (through persuasion / relationship) to enable and effect decision-making or take lead and make decision by him/herself.
MBTI	Altered your communication/thinking/presentation style to be more effective with someone else whose preferred style differed from your own.	Understanding of the different needs/preferences of Introverts/Extroverts (written, thinking-dependent vs. in-the-moment interpersonal communication), Sensing/Intuitive (detail vs. big picture), Thinking/Feeling (logic vs. emotion-/values-based decision-making), and Judging/Perceiving (time-bound vs. free flowing world order).

Appendix E | Methods of Enneagram Type Identification ("Typing")

Should the contents of this book have piqued the reader's interest in determining his/her own Enneagram type, there are many methods available to do so.

As with any self-assessment tool, it is always up to the individual to determine, confirm, and decide to divulge his/her own type to others. Of course, the efficacy of this determination is totally dependent on the person's level of self-awareness and ability to self-reflect objectively. In embarking on your journey of self-discovery and development, you may consider:

- Books: Plenty of books abound on how to determine one's Enneagram type. One of my perennial favorites continues to be David Daniels and Virginia Price's *The Essential Enneagram*, with its nine paragraphs assessment. The assessee reads nine paragraphs (in jumbled order) and selects the three to four which best describe and represent his/her worldview. Then, the reader consults with resources in the back of the book, where differentiating questions assist him/her in narrowing down his/her choices to the one that fits just right. This is best facilitated by an experienced Enneagram teacher who can spot the patterns and connections in the subject's selections and dive deeper into the differentiators and true motivations between them.
- Panels: One of the most powerful ways to determine

one's Enneagram type is to experience the interaction of a group of same-type individuals. This is especially poignant when a skilled Enneagram facilitator asks the panel members questions that tend to highlight how their experiences of certain situations differ from how other Enneagram types may experience those same situations. When the observer finds him/herself empathically agreeing, relating, and sympathizing with the panel members' answers and perspectives, then s/he realizes that s/he has come home and discovered his/her probable type. This is best experienced live and in person, at conferences or educational workshops, but can also be achieved by watching videos of such panel interactions.

- Online Instruments: Although we already stated that each person is the ultimate arbiter of his/her own Enneagram type, we all sometimes need some additional (read: outside) help. This is where proven and validated online assessments come into play. One of the most valid is Integrative Enneagram Solutions's Integrative Enneagram Questionnaire (IEQ). It can be accessed at www.integrative9.com. Other popular, validated web-based assessments include Don Riso and Russ Hudson's Riso-Hudson Enneagram Type Indicator (RHETI), accessible at www.enneagraminstitute.com/discover, and Jerry Wagner's Wagner Enneagram Personality Style Scales (WEPSS), accessed at www.wepss.com.

- Enneagram Teachers and Coaches: The International

Enneagram Association (IEA) manages a certification process and tracks their accredited Enneagram professionals. "Accredited Professionals" are IEA members who have attained a level of advanced knowledge/experience in using the Enneagram within their designated professional field and/or for teaching the Enneagram. These members have also agreed to adhere to the IEA's Ethical Guidelines and Code of Ethics. The IEA maintains this list at www.internationalenneagram.org. These teachers and coaches use a variety of instruments – including interviews, surveys, online assessment tools, and typing sort cards – to help coachees identify and confirm their Enneagram type.

While some people identify their Enneagram type soon after being introduced to the system, for many others it may become a lifelong search and discovery mission. Some may even initially identify with one Enneragram type and then, after undergoing deeper inquiry and work, realize that they may have mistyped themselves. As with any coaching engagement, it is always more meaningful and actionable when the subject him/herself comes to the realization and epiphany of his/her type and commits to the self-development work that aligns to it.

For a "quick-and-dirty" self-assessment to help guide the selection of Enneagram type (while calling out each type's strengths and unique differentiators), check out Appendix A.

Appendix F | Facilitation Success Guidelines

FACILITATION STEP / ACTION	LEVERAGE & CHANNEL THE ENERGY OF ENNEATYPE(S)
Disseminate agendas before first meeting (time, date, materials, links, logistics) so that everyone knows what to expect/prepare for optimal participation.	5, 6
Make it fun and exciting, i.e., have appropriate, theme-relevant upbeat music playing to set the tone.	7
Provide opportunity for participants to check in, get grounded, get to know each other, network, and connect (introductions, icebreakers, team-building exercises for longer-term engagements).	2, 9
Review the overall goal/value proposition/intention: What is the goal/objective of the session to help move towards that goal? Clarify for all participants.	1, 3
Co-create, gain agreement on, or review the meeting norms. Remind meeting participants that each is empowered/expected to maintain them.	1
Continuously scan to read the energy and engagement in the room ... and respond accordingly.	9
Ask open-ended, engaging, coaching questions, designed to draw out the insights of the participants.	5
Keep to the time, and allow for the flexibility to dive deeper and spend more time on important/impactful topics that arise, with everyone's agreement to change the agenda if necessary.	3, 7
Create and maintain a safe space for everyone to participate.	6, 9
Silence is OK, create space for people to think before speaking (especially important for introverts), i.e., writing thoughts on sticky notes, in chat, Jamboard, etc.	4, 5, 9
Consider diversity needs of the individual participants – draw out the diverse perspectives and the perspectives of traditionally underrepresented identities in the dominant culture.	4
Be impartial, as much as possible. If it becomes necessary to also contribute as a participant, be explicit about the temporary – and very short - change in your role.	9
Ensure that everyone gets equitable attention and opportunity (don't play favorites!).	1, 9
Keep track of participation, and invite less vocal participants to contribute/express their opinions ... but don't pressure. Step Forward, Step Back.	6, 9
Ensure psychological safety. Agree to keep discussion items in the "room" and between participants, unless all agree to share; share the learning/theme, not the personal/confidential details.	6
Implement ~10-minute breaks every 60 minutes, or 15-minute breaks every 90 minutes for longer meetings. Include stretch exercises, if possible/acceptable.	9
Keep track of agreements, parking lot items, and next steps. Ensure that each next step is clear, has an owner, and a deadline, along with a mechanism for follow-up.	8
Capture and communicate observations and themes.	5
Provide closure: opportunity for participants to check out about how they are each feeling (i.e., one word) and provide feedback on the meeting.	2, 3, 5, 9
Send any notes, documents, agreements, next steps, next agenda after each meeting. Confirm meeting cadence and availability/commitment of participants.	5, 8

Table of Figures

Figure 2-1 | The Johari Window

Figure 2-2 | What Motivates People?

Figure 2-3 | Motivators, Demotivators, and Team Value-Add by Enneagram Type

Figure 2-4 | Maslow Revisited

Figure 3-1 | Enneagram-Related Employment Decision Factors, $P<0.05$

Figure 3-2 | Enneagram-Related Employment Decision Factors, $0.05<P<0.08$

Figure 3-3 | Rules of Engagement by Enneagram Type

Figure 4-1 | Enneagram-Driven Strategic Planning Model

Figure 4-2 | SMART Goal Formula

Figure 4-3 | Enneagram-Driven Strategic Planning Flow

Figure 5-1 | The Urgent/Important Matrix

Figure 6-1 | Figure 6-1 | Enneagram Applied to Culture, Companies, and Countries

Figure 7-1 | Enneagram-Infused Kepner-Tregoe Decision-Making Matrix

Figure 9-1 | DiSC and Enneagram Correlates

Figure 9-2 | Enneagram Types Plotted on DiSC Axes

Figure 10-1 | Executive Coaching Focus Areas

Figure 10-2 | Hogan Personality Inventory and Enneagram Correlates

Figure 10-3 | Hogan Derailers and Enneagram Correlates

Figure 10-4 | Stakeholder Analysis Matrix

Figure 10-5 | Power/Influence Matrix

Figure 10-6 | Enneagram Styles and Related Reactive Fears and Creative Virtues

Figure 10-7 | Leadership Circle Profile Creative Behaviors and Reactive Tendencies by Enneagram Type

Figure 10-8 | Leadership Circle Profile Verbatim Themes by Enneagram Type

Figure 11-1 | Myers-Briggs Type Instrument and Enneagram Correlates

Figure 11-2 | Animals and Vehicles Correlated to the Enneagram

Figure 11-3 | Team Enneagram Type Strengths, Growth, and Hot Buttons

Figure 12-1 | Cutler & Purcell Grief/Loss/Change Process by Enneagram Type

Figure 12-2 | The Enneatypes in Isolation

Figure 13-1 | RACI/RASCIO Matrix

Figure 14-1 | Thomas-Kilmann Conflict Mode Instrument (TKI) and Enneagram Correlates

Figure 15-1 | Galbraith's Star Model

Appendix A | You Know You're Accessing Enneagram Type … If/When …

Appendix B | Enneagram Types, Subtypes, Counter-Types, & Look-Alikes

Appendix C | The Enneagram with MBTI, DiSC, and Body Center Correlates

Appendix D | Behavioral Interview Questions to Assess Emotional Intelligence

Appendix F | Facilitator Readiness Guidelines

References and Additional Resources

Alessandra, T. & O'Connor, M.J. (1996). *The Platinum Rule: Discover the Four Basic Business Personalities – And How They Can Lead You to Success.* New York, NY: Warner Books, Inc.

Anderson, R.J. & Adams, W.A. (2015). *Mastering Leadership: An Integrated Framework for Breakthrough Performance and Extraordinary Business Results.* Hoboken, NJ: Wiley.

Bast, M. & Thompson, C. (2014). *Out of the Box Coaching with the Enneagram.* Portland, OR: Stellar Attractions, Inc.

Chernick, S. (2016). The Connection between Personality Type and Conflict Style: A Deeper Look into Predicting Relationship Dynamics (Master's thesis, Notre Dame de Namur University, 2007).

Chernick-Fauvre, K. (2015, September). *Transformation Through Insight, Exploring the Meanings of the 2014 Enneagram Type, Tritype, Instinct, and MBTI Research Study Findings.* European Enneagram Conference, Copenhagen, Denmark.

Chestnut, B. (2013). *The Complete Enneagram: 27 Paths to Greater Self-Knowledge.* Berkeley, CA: She Writes Press.

Chestnut, B. (2015, September). *27 Subtypes: Using Knowledge of the Naranjo Subtypes for Personal Transformation.* European Enneagram Conference, Copenhagen, Denmark.

Chestnut, B. (2017). *The 9 Types of Leadership: Mastering the Art of People in the 21st Century Workplace.* Nashville, TN: Post Hill Press.

Cloete, D. & Greeff, L. (2014). *Understanding the Integrative Enneagram: Module 1, 2, 3, 4 Workbook.* Cape Town, South Africa: Integrative Enneagram Solutions.

Cloete, D. (2019). *Integrative Enneagram for Practitioners.* South Africa: ABC Press.

Colina, T. (1998, September/October). *Nine Ways of Looking at Work.* The Journal for Quality & Participation, 21(5), 56 – 59.

Connors, R., Smith, T., & Hickman, C. (2010). *The Oz Principle: Getting Results through Individual and Organizational Accountability.* New York, NY: The Penguin Group.

Covey, S., Merrill, A.R., & Merrill, R.R. (1994). *First things First: To Live, To Love, To Learn, To Leave a Legacy.* New York, NY: Simon & Schuster, Inc.

The How and Why: Taking Care of Business With The Enneagram

Cutler, J. & Purcell, A. (2015, May). *The Enneagram: Charting Your Course From Grief and Loss to a New Beginning.* Canadian Enneagram Conference, Toronto, Canada.

de Lange, M., (October 11, 2019). The Conscious Practice of Leadership Using the Enneagram and the Leadership Circle, International Enneagram Conference: The Art and Science of Consciousness, Cape Town, South Africa.

Daniels, D. & Price, V. (2000). *The Essential Enneagram: The Definitive Personality Test and Self-Discovery Guide.* San Francisco, CA: HarperCollins.

Ellis, A. & Ellis, D.J. (2011). *Rational Emotive Behavioral Therapy.* Washington, DC: American Psychological Association.

Galbraith, J.R. (1977). *Organization Design.* Reading, MA: Addison-Wesley.

Goldberg, M.J. (1999). *The 9 Ways of Working: How to Use the Enneagram to Discover Your Natural Strengths and Work More Effectively.* New York, NY: Marlowe & Company.

Goldsmith, M. & Reiter, M. (2007). *What Got You Here Won't Get You There: How Successful People Become Even More Successful.* New York, NY: Hyperion Books.

Goleman, D. (1995). *Emotional Intelligence: Why it can matter more than IQ*. New York, NY: Bantam Dell.

Grant, A. (2015, December 19). *The One Question you should ask about every new job*. NY Times.

Havens, S.E. *Comparisons of Myers-Briggs and Enneagram types of Registered Nurses*, M.S.N. 1995, University of Florida College and Nursing, 64pp.

Hebenstreit, R.K. (2007). *Using the Enneagram to Help Organizations Attract, Motivate, and Retain their Employees* (Doctoral dissertation, California School of Professional Psychology, 2007).

Hersey, P.H., Blanchard, K.H., & Johnson, D.E. (2012). *Management of Organizational Behavior*. 10th Ed. Upper Saddle River, NJ: Prentice Hall.

Hogan, R., Hogan, J., & Warrenfeltz, R. (2007). *The Hogan Guide: Interpretation and Use of the Hogan Inventories*. Tulsa, OK: Hogan Assessments, Inc.

Horney, K. (1945). *Our Inner Conflicts*. New York, NY: W.W. Norton & Co.

Horney, K. (1950). *Neurosis and Human Growth*. New York, NY: W.W. Norton & Co.

Isaacs, A. (2010, July). *Increasing Emotional Intelligence with EnneaMotion.* International Enneagram Association Annual Conference, San Francisco, CA.

Jones, T. & Brinkert, R. (2007). *Conflict Coaching: Conflict Management Strategies and Skills for the Individual.* Thousand Oaks, CA: Sage Publications.

Kepner, C.H. & Tregoe, B.B. (2013). *The New Rational Manager.* Princeton, NJ: Princeton Research Press.

Knowles, R.N. (2002). *The Leadership Dance: Pathways to Extraordinary Organizational Effectiveness, 3rd Ed.* Niagara Falls, NY: The Center for Self-Organizing Leadership.

Kübler-Ross, E. (1969). *On Death and Dying.* London, England: Routledge.

Lapid-Bogda, G. (2004). *Bringing out the Best in Yourself at Work: How to Use the Enneagram System for Success.* New York, NY: McGraw-Hill.

Lapid-Bogda, G. (2007). *What Type of Leader Are You? Using the Enneagram System to Identify and Grow Your Leadership Strengths and Achieve Maximum Success.* New York, NY: McGraw-Hill.

Lapid-Bogda, G. (2010). *Bringing out the Best in Everyone You Coach: Use the Enneagram System for Exceptional Results.* New York, NY: McGraw-Hill.

Lencioni, P. (2002). *The Five Dysfunctions of Teams: A Leadership Fable.* San Francisco, CA: Jossey-Bass.

Luft, J. (1969). *Of Human Interaction: The Johari Model.* San Francisco, CA: Mayfield Publishing Company.

Marston, W. M. (2015). *Emotions of Normal People.* Torquay, Great Britain: Devonshire Press.

Maslow, A.H. (1943). *A Theory of Human Motivation.* Psychological Review, 50.

Micka, C. (2012, July). *Conflict Management and the Enneagram: Implications for Managing Conflict with Family and Loved Ones.* International Enneagram Association Global Conference, Long Beach, CA.

O'Connor, J.M. & Anderson, B.M. (2003, August). *Shifting Universes – From Conflict to Resolution.* International Enneagram Association Conference, Santa Monica, CA.

Palmer, H. & Brown, P.B. (1997). *The Enneagram Advantage: Putting the 9 Personality Types to Work in the Office.* New York, NY: Three Rivers Press.

Patterson, K., Grenny, J., McMillan, R., & Switzler, A. (2002). *Crucial Conversations: Tools for Talking When Stakes Are High.* New York, NY: McGraw-Hill.

Phipps Senft, L. (2012). Self-Awareness and Conflict Transformation: The Enneagram as a Catalyst. Baltimore, MD: Baltimore Mediation.

Pink, D.H. (2011). Drive: The Surprising Truth About What Motivates Us. New York, NY: Penguin Group.

Rohr, R. & Ebert, A. (2001). The Enneagram: A Christian Perspective. Chestnut Ridge, NY: Crossroad Publishing Company.

Ronsick, B. & Wyman, P. (August 15, 2019). Bringing the Enneagram into LCP Coaching Engagements. Retrieved from https://leadershipcircle.com/en/bringing-the-enneagram-into-lcp-coaching-engagements/

Scott, S. (2002). Fierce Conversations: Achieving Success at Work and in Life One Conversation at a Time. New York, NY: Berkley Publishing Group.

Schein, E. (1985). Organizational Culture and Leadership. San Francisco, CA: Jossey-Bass.

Sikora, M. & Tallon, R. (2006). Awareness to Action. Scranton, PA: University of Scranton Press.

Sikora, M. (2007, August). Overcoming Resistance to Change: Performance Improvement and the Inner Triangle. International Enneagram Association Conference, Redwood City, CA.

Thomas, K.W. & Kilmann, R.H. (2002). Thomas-Kilmann Conflict Mode Instrument. Palo Alto, CA: CPP, Inc.

Torgal, E. (2014, April). The New Paradigm Challenges. European Enneagram Conference, Carcavelos, Portugal.

Tuckman, B. (1965). Developmental sequence in small groups. Psychological Bulletin 63 (6): 384 – 99.

The How and Why: Taking Care of Business With The Enneagram

www.AperianGlobal.com

www.beatricechestnut.com

www.cpp.com

www.EnneagramCentral.com

www.EnneagramCoachAndMentor.blogspot.com

www.EnneagramHQ.com

www.EnneagramInstitute.com

www.executiveenneagram.com

www.HayGroup.com

www.HoganAssessments.com

www.integrative9.com

www.integroleadership.com

www.internationalenneagram.org

www.Kepner-Tregoe.com

www.mundoeneagrama.com

www.n-1games.com

www.NineDomains.com

www.PerformAndFunction.com

www.personalitycafe.com/enneagram-personality-theory-forum/160857-enneagram-disc-interaction-styles-social-styles.html

www.SergiConsulting.com

www.TheEnneagramInBusiness.com

www.wepss.com

Made in the USA
Las Vegas, NV
31 May 2023